Decision Making

Impact of Impulse

Makarand Arvind Paithankar

First made in USA in 2017 by

CreateSpace, USA

ISBN-13: 978-1541343733

ISBN-10: 1541343735

Made by

CreateSpace

4900 LaCross Road

North Charleston, SC29406

USA

First print January 2017

CONTENTS

PREFACE

"What a piece of work is man! How noble in reason! How infinite in faculty! In form, in moving, how express and admirable! In action how like an angel! In apprehension how like a God! The beauty of the world! The paragon of animals!"

Shakespeare,
Hamlet-Act II Scene II

Further Hamlet says, *"And yet to me, what is this quintessence of dust? Man delights not me."*

'Human nature' may not have changed since Shakespearean era, but the world today we are living in is even more complicated and complex and crowded. About the first thing we do to identify people today is to find out the principal organization of which they are members. It is no exaggeration to say that we are living in the age of the organizational man. A man who accepts the organizational goals as the value premises of his decision, tending to make their behaviour 'organization' In recent years it has resulted into the study of behaviour and attitudes of persons working in them. The enormous growth and impact of science and technology has further complicated the administration.

An organization is a unique living organism whose basic component is the individual. Organization is a structure of decision makers in which, all the administrative functions boil down to one point that is decision making. The behaviour of the respective organization and administration depends upon the decision making skills of an individual. Decision making is the act of determining own mind upon an opinion or course of action. It is selection based on criteria of one behaviour alternative from two or more available alternatives. If there is no choice there is no decision to be made. The decision is based on some criteria or basis believed important in particular situation. It represents a choice from a group of alternatives which one feels best for particular situation or state of affairs. It is simple to state that alternatives are evaluated in terms of their probable outcomes but to determine the relative merits is usually difficult. The requirement is to make comparison based on values be they economic, social, psychological or political. Conflict among these values is quite likely. There are normally both desirable and undesirable aspects in every alternative but these conflicting values must be reconciled in some satisfactory manner.

An individual's impulses affects their choice of values, their impulses are not fixed from the beginning by their native disposition. They are profoundly modified by their circumstances and their way of life. Impulse is at the basis of human activity. It is not any purpose but merely an impulse that prompts such actions as quarrelling, boasting, etc. We all believe many things which we have no good reason for believing because subconsciously our nature craves certain kinds of action which this belief would render reasonable if they were true. The unfound beliefs are the homage which impulse pays to reasons and thus with the beliefs which opposite but similar make individuals believe it their duty to act.

In this book of mine attempt is made to empirically present the interrelatedness, interactions and impact of impulse on decision making and how it influences the administrative working and processes. I hope this will add to the plethora of literature available on administrative behaviour. It was cerebrally satisfying experience for me to understand and present not only the psychological aspects but physiological basis of impulse and decision making. Hope you will appreciate the attempt.

I am indebted to large numbers of scholars and authors upon whose writings I have largely drawn. To those who took the trouble to read the manuscript and offer comments I am grateful. I would like to thank my Management and Principal where I work; and to colleagues and friends, discussions with whom have always enriched my points of view. Thanks to CreateSpace for taking up this work.

Finally I thank my wife Smita and son Raghav for their continued support and help.

DECISION MAKING: THEORY AND PROCESSES

> *Ultimately all decisions are made on the basis of judgements. There is no other way and there never will be. The question is whether those judgements have to be made in the fog of inadequate and inaccurate data, unclear and undefined issues and a welter of conflicting personal opinions or whether they can be made on the basis of adequate reliable information, relevant experience, and clearly drawn issues. In the end, analysis is but an aid to judgement ... Judgement in supreme.*
>
> —Alain C. Enthoven

Meaning

Etymologically the verb 'decide' is derived from the Latin Prefix 'de' meaning 'off' and the word 'caedo' meaning 'to cut'. In this sense some cognitive process cuts off or cuts short as preferred alternatives. It is frequently used to mean reaching a conclusion' or 'making up our minds'. In decision making, totality of human mind is involved in decision making: (i) cognition – those activities of mind associated with knowledge; (ii) conation – the action of mind, implied by such words as 'willing', 'desire' and 'aversion'; and (iii) affectation - the aspects of mind indentified with emotion, feeling mood and temperament.[1] Based on these facts decision making has been defined as 'a conscious and human process involving both individual and social phenomenon based upon factual and value premises, which concludes with a choice of one behavioural activity from among one or more alternatives with the intention of moving toward some state of affairs.'[2] Decision making is fundamental to organism and organisation behaviour. Decision making is at the core of administration. Decision making is central activity of administration. It involves what is to be done, who is to do it, when, where and how to do it. Decision making permeates through all administrative functions. All matters relating to planning, organizing, directing, staffing and controlling are settled through decisions. Decision – Making allows coherence in systems. "The living systems are a special subset of the set of all possible concrete systems, composed of the plants and the animals. They all have the following characteristics (among others): They are open systems...They contain a decider, the essential critical subsystem which controls the entire system, causing its subsystems and components to act, without which there is no system."[3] We make personal and administrative \ organisational decisions endlessly, which dress should I wear? How should I respond to press? Where shall we eat lunch?

Shall we able to pump up resources for a newly launched corporation? And so on throughout the day.

Thinking, problem solving and decision making are fundamental to human behaviour. Decision making is important task in organisation endeavour towards achieving goals.

Complexity: The Context of Decision Making

The environmental context in which organisation exists are themselves changing at an increasing rate and towards increasing complexity.[4] Alvin Toffler in Future shock suggests the turbulence in modern societies. "The acceleration of change in our time is itself, an elemental force. This accelerative thrust has personal and psychological, as well as sociological consequences... future shock are a time phenomenon, a product of the greatly accelerated rate of change in society. It arises from the superimposition of a new culture, on an old one. It is culture shock in one's own society.[5]

The decision makers are affected by the dynamism and uncertainty of internal organisational climate and the external environment within which it functions. It makes impossible to mould all the variables that administration considers important into structured (well – defined) models that can be quantified and solved.

The following figure depicting three concentric circles show the picture of decision making which is complex process. Every human being living in a society is affected by societal norms, which matches his behaviour or near (close to it).

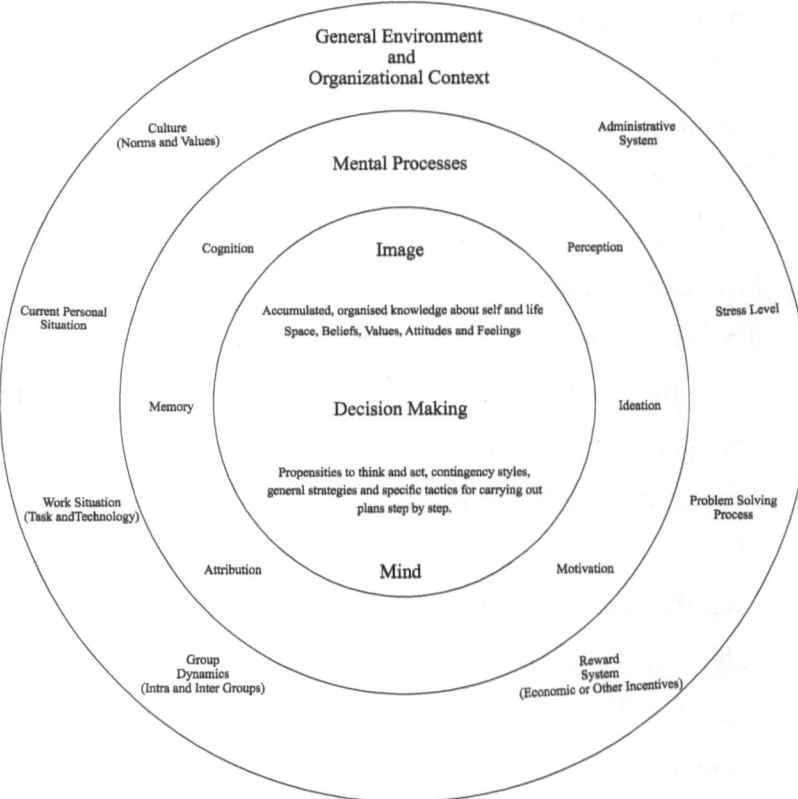

Figure 1.1
Contextual factors (potential) affecting decision making and behaviour

Specific choice making is one of the major functions when one works in an organisation, for example in group dynamics intra-group and intergroup relationship affects decision making. In reward system, choice is to be made on economic incentives or other incentives. In work situation task and technology have their demands and constraints which affects the decision. In between the 'general organisation environment', and the 'mind of decision maker' is the 'mental processes' which is in between the actual situation and our image. Perception, cognition, attribution helps to create personal opinion of a problem or situation, resulting in decision making and behaviour which one considers appropriate in particular situation. At the core of figure is the mind of decision maker. It interacts with environment and provides an up to date image in particular situation. This results in natural inclination to think and act in certain ways in certain situations.

The decision making process sometimes include thoroughly formulated or developed situations. However many premises and constraints are 'in the mind' of the decision maker.[7]

Rationality

Rationality is a state characterised by reasonableness. Rationality may be defined as the capacity for objective and intelligent action. There is a patent behavioural nexus between ends and means. If appropriate means are chosen to reach desired ends, the decision is perfectly rational. Herbert Simon denies the possibility of assuming the 'total rationality' of decisions. He thinks it is based on following 'unrealistic assumptions.'

- The decision makers 'omniscience' concerning the existence of all possible alternatives and their future consequences or the probability distribution of consequences.
- His unlimited computational ability.
- His carrying in his head a 'complete and consistent preference ordering' of all possible consequences.

Simon rejects such assumptions, stating that 'actual human rationality' is neither perfectly rational nor irrational. There are number of ways to view rationality. "A decision may be called 'objectively' rational if in fact it is the correct behaviour for maximising given values in a given situation. It is 'subjectively' rational if it maximises attainment relative to the actual knowledge of the subject. It is 'consciously' rational to the degree that the adjustment of means to ends is a 'consciously' rational to the degree that the adjustment of means to ends is a conscious process. It is 'deliberately' rational to the degree that the adjustment of means to ends has been deliberately brought about (by the individual or by the organisation). A decision is 'organisationally' rational if it is oriented to the individual's goals".[8] 'Bounded rationality' is associated with Herbert Simon. Bounded rationality is a

6

particular characteristic of human decision making under conditions of extreme complexity. In the face of complex and uncertain situations one cannot behave in a totally rational manner, because the information processing capacity of a person is too limited to encompass all the knowledge required for decision making. Bounded rationality describes man as a decision maker who confines the situation by bounding or limiting the amount of data to be dealt with – often in imaginative and creative manner and then behaving in rational fashion with this limited data base.

In bounded rationality and out of the infinite number of possible alternatives, people analyses few and predicts few and in doing so makes few mistakes. Simon also points out that the 'aspiration level' as such is not something stable and immutable. The aspiration level rises when the individual in his exploration of alternatives discovers satisfactory alternatives. His aspiration level falls when he finds it difficult to discover the satisfactory alternatives. Thus, instead of optimizing upon the solution or alternatives one is satisfied with decisions that are 'good enough' since one has no wit to 'maximise' is compelled to 'satisfice'. By this organisation also compensate for the limited rationality of individuals.

Programmed and Non-Programmed

Again, it was Herbert Simon, the Nobel laureate, who distinguished decisions into two types, programmed and non-programmed.

Programmed decisions are routine and repetitive in nature. Programmed decisions are applied to structured problems. It relies on pre-established criteria or notion. Programmed decision making is decision making by antecedent. Programmed decision making is regular routine application of established rules and regulation to individual cases. Processing of application forms for admissions in university can be cited as an example of establish specific guidelines or a processing system for handling the applications.

Non-Programmed decisions are novel unstructured, consequential and ill-defined situations of a non – recurring nature. A non programmed decision is called for because no tried and tested method of handling the 'situation arisen' is available or because of the evasive, complicated and unpredictable nature of the situation. Non programmed decision requires subjective judgements.

Most decisions are neither black nor white, they are grey; they are neither completely programmed nor completely non-programmed. Non programmed decisions are taken at upper level of administration because senior level bureaucrats or

8

executives have to deal with unstructured problems. They have to face or tackle the contingency, comparatively lower level of organisation have problems and work of routine and repetitive nature. Selection and training of executives possessing higher skills, innovative ability, creativity, etc., are techniques to deal with non programmed decisions while programmed decisions requires habit, skills, knowledge, etc. The following figure shows the programmed and non programmed decision making in an organisation and the problems faced by it.

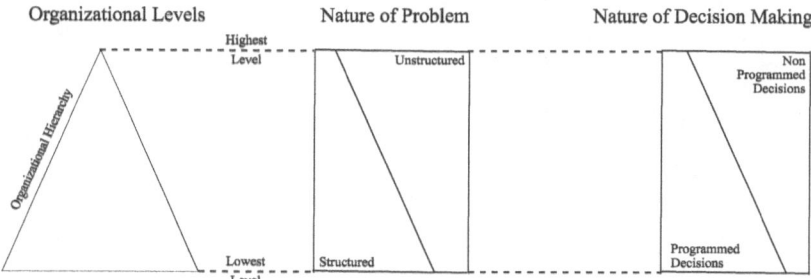

Figure 1.2
Nature of problems and decision making in the organisation.[9]

Decision Making Process

Decision making process contains four basic phases: "The First Phase of the decision making process – searching the environment for the conditions calling for decision – I shall call intelligence activity.

The Second Phase – inventing, developing and analysing possible courses of action – I shall call design activity.

9

The Third Phase – selecting a particular course of action from those available – I shall call choice activity.

The Fourth Phase – assessing past choices. I shall call review activity."[10]

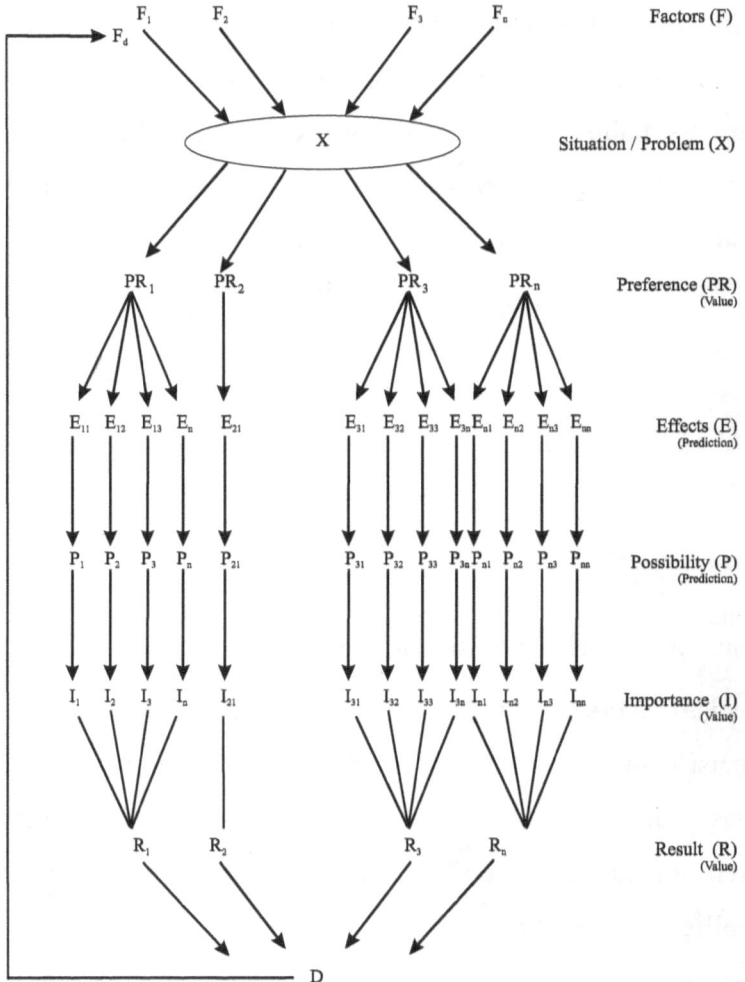

Figure 1.3
The Decision Making Process

The classification of decision making process into phases is very useful for understanding what happens and how it happens even though the activities undertaken in doing it are not guarded completely. They are vulnerable of internal and external organisation factors. There are number of problem in the air. The activity undertaken for designing alternative courses of action may create additional problems which results in repeating of new intelligence activity. The continuous decision cycles might contain a series of such sub cycles.

The decision making process is shown in figure. There are number of factors that affect the problem and the decision maker. These factors are external and some are internal to decision maker. The beliefs and values of decision maker effect the decision making process.

The next step involves prediction of future effects of preferences. This may be objective or subjective depending on the degree of uncertainties involved. The possibilities may be verified with the help of past experience. For a unique complex problem where data is not available, the prediction is subjective and speculative. The decision makers anticipates the future by own judgement of the situation, it may be consciously or unconsciously, objectively or subjectively.

After the assessment of effects and possibilities of each outcomes, the decision maker than consider a particular outcome. If it has a utility it is of great help in the decision process. After weighting the preferences by its importance the decision maker chooses and feeds back into environment of subsequent decision. The above process or other similar to it followed in non routine and unstructured situations.

Approaches to Decision Making

There is neither one best approach nor one combination for decision making which can be used in all situations. The selection is individual and depends upon the decision makers background and knowledge and the available resources. There is no 'one best way' for decision making because it is basically situational or contingent. As Robbins has stated "… OB (Organisational Behaviour) concepts are founded on situational conditions; that is, if X, than Y, but only conditions specified in Z (the contingency variable ….)"[11]. The effectiveness of decision approaches or styles is contingent upon the situation in which it is used.

The most effective decision makers not only have the diagnostic ability to determine the most appropriate decision but also have the ability to correctly apply that style. Ralph Stogdill put it best when he said the most effective decision makers "appear to exhibit a degree of versatility and flexibility that enables them to adapt their behaviour to the changing and contradictory demands made on them".[12]

12

There are as many decision style and models as are scholars and writers on subject. This does not in any way curtails its significance. Even *'Arthashastra'* ancient Indian classic indentifies three bases for information acquisition. These include, the 'directly perceived', the 'unperceived' and the 'inferred'.[13] Accordingly, decision making is based on these three types of information. The multitude of models and styles of decision making only points to its importance. For practical convenience many of this models and styles are grouped into two approaches, quantitative; and non quantitative.

Quantitative Bases

The quantitative techniques are of great importance in administrative decision making as it brings maximum rationality to it. The emphasis of quantitative techniques is on means or how best to accomplish the stated objective. The quantitative techniques involve problem conception, hypothesis, definition and experiment. The probability arrived at is of great importance and is well defined. The processing towards the final decision is rational. Uniformity of behaviour is assumed and rational predictions and logical explanations are utilised. Some of the important quantitative bases in use are operations research, linear programming, gaming etc.

Operations Research (OR) - The term operations research was coined by McClosky and Treythen of UK. It was during

Second World War, the military management in England called upon a team of scientist to assist in solving strategic and tactical problems related to improvement in execution of various military projects. Operations research was apparently invented, as the team was dealing with research on operations (military).

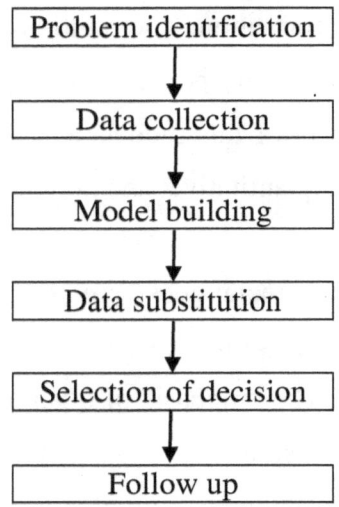

Figure 1.4
The steps in operations research

Operations research consists of data collection on specific problem, tabulation, processing and analysing these data. Then it resolves quantitative reports on relative advantages of a potential course of action. In doing so concepts of optimization, input-output and mathematical model are used.

The problem best suited for operations research involves recurring decision and concerning to time, cost, profit or anything which can be optimised.

14

Linear Programming- Linear programming is a technique for determining an optimum schedule of interdependent activities in view of the available resources. Linear programming is decision technique which optimises the available resources for the realization of organisational goals. The application of linear programming requires certain conditions.

- An objective is to be optimised either maximum output or minimum inputs is sought which can be expressed in terms of profits or costs, time or quantity. This is the condition of 'constrained optimization'.
- The relationship between the various forces and the outcome should be linear or in a straight line i.e. if a = 2 then 2a will be 4.
- Restrictions on the relationships of the forces exist, without the restriction the linear programming would be unnecessary.

The computation is by means of 'iteration' – a method of repetition which determines at the end of every step what the next will be. This helps in getting closer to the best option available. This technique makes use of matrix algebra or linear equations of mathematics.

Simulation- Simulation is a systematic 'trial and error' approach to the complex problem. The idea of simulation is to create a virtual reality for carrying the experiment to observe

15

the effect of various forces on the final results. Simulation creates an abstraction of reality to observe the influences that affect it in reality. Simulation makes it possible to trace the activities as relationships and various forces change. Simulation models are empirical, quantitative representation of behavioural characteristics, interactions and non-logical features of the subject under study.

Queuing Theory- Whenever a 'service' is required and it has to be taken up in sequence with some priority rules, the item or person may have to wait before the service for the same is taken up. The queue is on account of lack of capability to serve them all at a time. The queues may be of persons waiting at post office or at railways booking office. In the absence of a perfect balance between the service facilities and service seekers there is lost time, unused labour, and excessive cost. To minimise the losses is the objective of queuing. Queuing is concerned with flow and includes the reconsideration of paper work, processes and of material handlings. This Technique involves the balancing expenditure of existing queues with the cost of providing additional facilities.

Queuing has shown that for 29 customers arriving randomly each hour at a post office stamp window with each customer taking 2 minutes to transact business there will be an average waiting line of 28 customers and an average wait of 58

16

minutes. If an additional stamp window is opened the average waiting line is reduced to less than 1 customer and by it 26 customer hours will be saved at the cost of one additional attendant. Queuing is also called as waiting line. Queuing theory is of great importance in administration where delay is considered as the enemy of efficiency and waiting is the enemy of utilization.

Gaming- In their book *Theory of Games and Economic Behaviour*, Von Neumann and Morgenstern have introduced the game theory. Gaming is the body of thought which deals with ration decision strategies in situation of conflicts and competition, where each participation or player seeks to maximise gains and minimise losses. In theory of games the strategy and decision of one actor depends on the decision and strategies of the other in the competitive situations. Though games theory relies heavily on mathematical models they are relatively simple since basic ratios, projections and statistics are used. Game theory is applicable to decision making where no independently 'best' alternative is available and the best outcome depends on what others do. The game theory is quite popular in international relations. A good example can be cited of U. S. and Russia on Cuban question.

Non Quantitative Bases

Non quantitative bases are considered by many as the natural way of making decisions. They are widely known and highly personal. The non quantitative bases are helpful in problem dealing with 'means' to achieve the 'end'. The most widely used non quantitative bases are intuition, facts, experience, considered opinions etc.

Intuition- Intuition is knowledge discerned directly by mind without reasoning or analysis. Intuition is a revelation arrived at by insight. The features of intuition are the use of hunches, inner feelings or gut feeling for decision making. The subjective element is very vital in intuitive decision making. Suggestions, influences, choice, values, likings or psyche of a person plays an important part in decision making. The intuitive decision maker is influenced, most probably by his subconscious memory which is not habitually utilised. Roy Rowan the 'Fortune' magazine writer cited as a study that found that more than 80 percent of top level managers who had doubled their company's profits within a five year span had above average intuitive skills.[14] The intuitive decision makers have the ability to 'see through' defies logic. Robert Jensen, Chairman, General Cable Crop., says "On each issue the mathematical analysis only got me to the point where my intuition had to take over."[15] The intuitive decision maker by their sheer conviction of beliefs and abilities to sense opportunity push forward the decisions. They usually are activist's moves fast, questions situations and finds solutions, rely on instincts and feelings. Intuitive thinker tend to keep the overall problem continuously in mind, redefine the problem frequently as they proceed, rely on verbalised cues even hunches, defend the solution in terms of fitness, consider a number of alternatives and options. Simultaneously jump from one step in analysis or search to another and back again, explore and abandon alternatives very quickly.[16] The intuitive decision makers thought process is conditioned by the values and experience.

Facts- A decision based on adequate facts is widely accepted. A decision based on facts enjoys a strong and sound footing. In this information era with the perceptibility of computers, there is greater emphasis on use of facts in decision making. A decision should be taken after diagnosis, classification, and interpretation of facts carefully. In doing this much attention should be given on imagination, experience and belief. Facts help in reducing the element of 'unknown' from any decision making technique that is followed but they don't eliminate it. "Facts", Aldous Huxley remarked, "are ventriloquists dummies sitting on wise man's knee may be made to utter words of wisdom; elsewhere they say nothing, or talk nonsense."[17]

Experience- The administrators can take the decision on the basis of their past experience. Experience is not what happens to you, it is what you do with what happens to you. Experience furnishes guides for decision making. It helps in solving the question of what to do in particular situation. Experience enables to recognise a mistake when one makes it again. Decisions based on experience utilize practical knowledge. The tried and tested portions of the decision maker's background are used. It also enjoys support of others. There are certain dangers in relying on ones past experience because very few persons recognise underlying causes of past failures and future is not the same as past and the experience may be totally unsuitable. The other thing is experience is a dim lamp which only lights the one who bears it. One cannot create experience, one must undergo it. The administrator should use experience but should not blindly bind by it.

Considered Opinions- Considered opinions make use of logic behind the decision. Considered opinion is a rational process though small for decision making. It makes use of statistics to make decision logical.

Decision Making under Certainty, Uncertainty and Risk

Decision making is the selection of alternative and the alternative is put into action which will take place in future. It is not a process of making future decisions but a means of reflecting the future in today's decision. It is process of 'present' which reflects 'future' in it. All decisions are made in an environment of at least some uncertainty and degree varies from relative certainty to great uncertainty along a continuum.

In a situation involving certainty administrator has sufficient information about all the variables that effects and gets affected by the decision. The conditions of certainty exist in routine and repetitive types of decisions when information is reliable and available and where cause and effect of relationship are known. In the situation of uncertainty the database available is very low and there is question of its authenticity and reliability. Under the conditions of uncertainty it is very difficult to develop probability estimates because it is difficult to gauge the likelihood of the various alternatives. It is difficult to evaluate the interactions of various variables. The various alternatives for making a decision in such cases are three. They are as follows

- Laplace Criterion – Since the occurrence of the events is not known equal probability can be applied to all states of nature of events.
- Max-min approach – is pessimist in nature. In this worst condition for each alternative is ascertained.
- Maxi-max approach – In this probability to various alternatives is optimistically assigned.

In condition of risk, the information is factual but it may be incomplete most of the organisation decisions are made under the conditions of risk. The information available is sufficient for probable estimation of outcomes, to estimate the objective probability mathematical models and for subjective probability judgement and experience are used. There are various techniques available which can be used for decision making under the condition of risk. Some of these are decision trees, simulation, etc.

Values and Beliefs- Decision making involves choice. It is selection of best possible alternative 'two kinds of judgements are involved in choice: evaluations and predictions, i.e. judgements of preference and belief.[18] For decision making both these aspects are important. Values represent basic convictions that 'a specific mode of conduct or end state of existence is personally or socially preferable to and opposite or converse mode of conduct or end state of existence.'[19] Values have judgemental content as it carries individuals notion about what is right, what is preferable or what should be? This value judgement has a significant role in decision making. Values contain interpretation of right and wrong. They (values) determine preference for specific behaviour or outcome. As a result it may hamper objectivity and rationality. It is an indispensable element of decision making.

Now the question about the sources of our value system arises, from where do our value systems come? The answer is significant portion of our values are innate i.e. 'born with'. These values are genealogical. Studies of twin reared apart demonstrate that about 40% of the variation in work values is explained by genetics.[20] The rest of the portion of values are established in our early years from parents, teachers, friends, national culture and social environmental influences. Interestingly, values are relatively stable and enduring.[21] This has been explained as a result of both their genetic component and the way in which they are learned.[22] For example as children we are told to be honest and hard worker. This is always desirable in its absolute sense not to be little honest and a bit hard worker. It is this complete either black or white learning of values with added genetics in it makes for its enduring, long lasting and stable nature. But as an individual grows up with his mature thinking, self assessment and questioning about the acceptability of values may bring in a change in values. Individuals convictions may remain same or it may change resulting in change in value 'Belief reflect an individual's view of the interrelationship of events either past, present or future'.[23] Belief are predictive judgements they are conviction or acceptance of something that is right and real. The only important difference between values (what is good) and belief (what is true) is that belief can be confirmed or disconfirmed. An individual's system of beliefs is collection overtime and tabulated continually according to experience. However 'peoples belief change slowly and is extraordinarily resistant to new information. Research in social psychology has often demonstrated that once formed, people's initial impressions tend to structure the way they interpret subsequent information. They give full weight to evidence that is consistent with their initial beliefs while dismissing contrary evidence as unreliable, erroneous, or unrepresentative.'[24]

Factors Influencing Decisions

The role which administrators play in an organisation guides their decision making. The decision making is influenced by the expectations others have of how they are expected to conduct and behave in accordance with what they are expected to behave by the organisation in which they are working. They have their respective roles to play but still role conflict takes place because of the differing expectations about the decisions a person should make. The influence of role perception is very noticeable when one changes position. For example a minister in charge of department of environment will try hard to conserve, protect and increase green cover in cities and may advocate control on industries. But the same person when becomes minister in charge of industries will be more concerned about industrial growth than clean air or green cover. This is because this new position provides for new perspective. So it is not a question of hypocrisy.[26] Nor do administrators change all their beliefs. When they shift to other position it stays as an internal role conflict when the administration is called to behave differently towards their former department. Sometimes administrators are forced to act in a particular manner because of the pressure groups which work from outside the organisation. Tenure system helps to ignore this pressure because of the security but still in some degree they have to yield. This is very obvious because of their role in public policy making, discretionary powers which they enjoy, value choices which they make, that proves their involvement in political process. It means that decision making procedures cannot be shaped independently of the real world. It needs a holistic approach.

The other factor which influences decision making is substantial amount of investment made on projects. Which appear to critics as useless or there is evidence of original faulty decision and it should be rectified but administrator persists with it. This 'sunk cost' explains governmental inertia and conservatism. Modes of conduct have been built around the existing policies and to undertake new one means much additional effort. The other factors which influence decision are previous training and previous work history.

References

1) **Fremont A. Shull, Jr., Andre L. Delbecq, and L. L. Cummings,** *Organisation Decision Making,* McGraw- Hill, New York, 1970, P. 30.

2) **Fremont A. Shull, Jr., Andre L. Delbecq, and L. L. Cummings,** *Organisation Decision Making,* McGraw- Hill, New York, 1970, P. 31

3) **Jame G. Miller,** *Living systems: Basic Concepts,* Behavioural Science, July 1965, P. 203, 204.

4) **F. E. Emery and E. L. Trist,** *The Causal Texture of organisation Environments,* Human Relations, February 1965, P. 21.

5) **Alvin Toffler,** *Future Shock,* Random house, New York, 1971, P. 2.

6) **Fremont E. Kast and James E. Rosenzweig,** *Organisation and Management,* McGraw – Hill, 1988, P. 454.

7) **Alvin Toffler,** Future shock, Random house, New York, 1971, P. 11.

8) **Herbert Simon,** *Administrative Behaviour,* The Free Press, New York, 1976, P. 76, 77.

9) **Harold Koontz, Heinz Weihrich,** *Management,* McGraw – Hill, 1988, P. 142.

10) **Herbert Simon,** *The new science of management decision,* Prentice Hall, 1977, P. 40, 41.

11) **Stephan Robbins,** *Organisational Behavior,* Prentice Hall, 7th Ed., 1996, P. 12.

12) **Ralph M. Stogdill,** *Historical Trends in Leadership Theory and Research,* Journal of Contemporary Business, Autumn, 1974, P. 7.

13) **R. P. Kangle,** *Arthashastra,* Motilal Banarasidass, Delhi, 1986, P. 33.

14) **Roy Rousan,** *Those Business Hunches are more than Blind faith,* Fortune, April 23, 1979, P. 111.

15) **Roy Rousan,** *Those Business Hunches are more than Blind faith,* Fortune, April 23, 1979, P. 112.

16) **James L. McKenny and Peter G. W. Keen,** *How Managers Minds Work,* Harvard Business Review, May-June, 1974, P. 83.

17) **Aldous Huxley,** *Time must have a stop,* 1945.

18) **Robin Hagarth,** *Judgement and Choice,* John Wiley and Sons, Inc., New York, 1980, P. 9.

19) **Rokeach. M.,** *The Nature of Human Values,* The Free Press, New York, 1973, P. 5.

20) **L. M. Keller, T. J. Bouchard, Jr., R. D. Arvey, N. L. Segal, and R. V. Dawis,** *Work Values: Genetic and Environmental Influences,* Journal of Applied Psychology, Feb. 1992, P. 79 – 88.

21) **M. Rokeach and S. J. Ball** – *Rokeach, Stability and Change in American Value Priorities,* 1968-81, American Psychologist, May, 1989, P. 775-784.

22)**M. Rokeach,** *The Nature of Human Values,* The Free Press, New York, 1973, P. 6.

23) **Ronald J. Ebert and Terence R. Mitchell,** *Organisational Decision Processes,* Crane Russak and Company, Inc., New York, 1975, P. 51.

24) **Paul Slovic, Baruch Fischoff, and Sarah Lichtenstein,** *Risky Assumptions,* Psychology Today, June, 1980. P. 48.

25) **Felix Nigro, Lloyd G. Nigro,** *Modern Public Administration*, Harper and Row Publishers, New York, 1989, P. 156.

26) **Cynthia He Enloe,** *The Politics of Pollution in a Comparative Perspective,* McKay, New York, 1975, P. 90.

THE CONTEXT OF DECISION MAKING

> *"Our main job today is learning how to make world safe for diversity."*
>
> - Norman Cousins.

The Ecology

The ecology and environment are used as synonyms. Decision making cannot take place in isolation. Decision making being a dynamic activity is always affected by its ecology. The ecology casts a direct and penetrating affect on the decision making. The term 'ecology' is borrowed from biology. The study of life and its surroundings is ecology. In the words of John M. Gaus, ecological approach "builds quite literally from the ground up from the elements of a place-soils, climate, location, for example; to the people who live there – their numbers and age and knowledge, and the way of physical and social technology by which from the place and in relationship with one another, they get their living".[1] The credit of popularising ecological approach goes to Fred W. Riggs. When he classified the societies based on his 'structure functional' approach. The structure is a behavioural pattern which plays a dynamic role in a system and the function is the role played by the system.

Riggsian theory is of immense importance. It would be difficult to find a student of public administration who shows ignorance about Fred W. Riggs.[2]

It is the social, cultural, geographical, economic, political, factors and individual attributes of the decision makers that affects the decision making. This is the environment in which decision making activity takes place. The figure 2.1 illustrates the environment of decision – making.

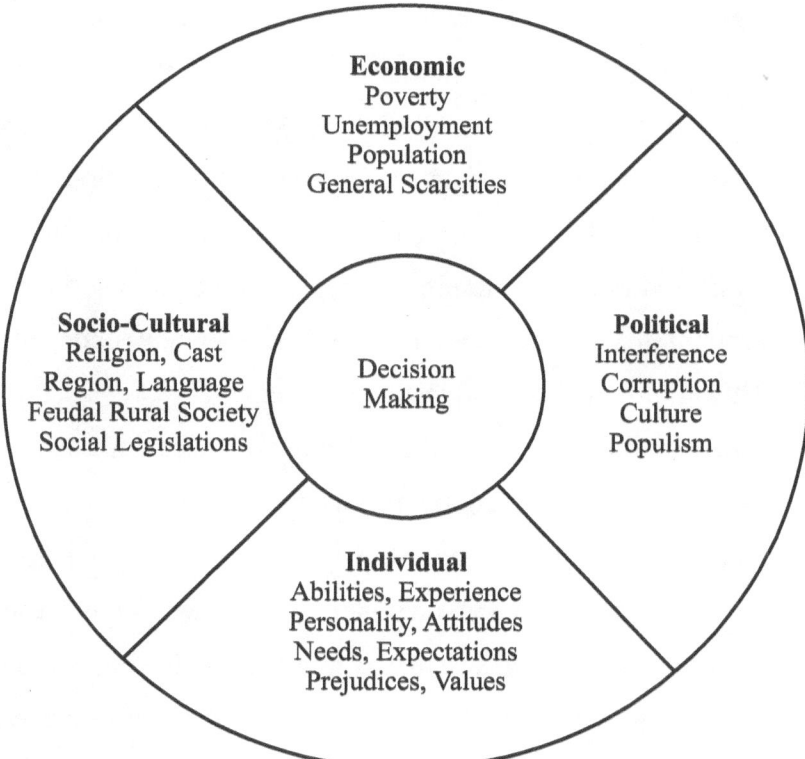

Figure 2.1
Ecology of Decision Making

Political Factors

It is the country's political system that creates its administrative system. Traditionally policy making has been the domain of politics and implementation of policies is the responsibility of administration. This is easier said than done. The politics and administration influence each other that make it impossible to demarcate the role played by them.

Political Interference- India has opted for the parliamentary democracy. In which the elected executive is accountable to the legislature. As a result ministers fall prey to the unreasonable demands of individual legislators. Ministers have to oblige them leading to undue interference in administration. In five decades working of Indian polity, most of the time we witnessed one party dominance rule which also to some extent brought the political neutrality of bureaucracy under stress. This in turn affects the decision making.

Political Culture- It is the politics which can make or mar nations because the politicians are the destiny builders of any nation. The political leadership which emerges in developing societies throws a very sorry picture of affairs. Ends are more important than the means. Their political culture is also reward benefit and the national interests are subordinated to individual interest. The political scene that emerges is of unprincipled normlessness without ethos and the intensity increases as one goes down to grass root levels. This has serious bearing on the decision making.

Populism- In developing nations planning is criticised as over ambitions. In elections political leaders take refuge to the populism without taking into account the practical concerns of the finance. The populism or populist policies affect the decision making and public administration of the country.

Corruption- In India according to Santhanam committee, 'Any action or failure to take action in the performance or duty by a government servant for some advantage is corruption.' Corruption involves;

  i) Misuse of official position or authority;

  ii) Deviation from rules, laws and norms;

  iii) Personal gain for selfish motives;

  iv) Monetary and non-monetary forms;

  v) Harm to public good; and

  vi) No action when action is required.

It is widely accepted that corruption is dysfunctional to the system of governance and to the society as a whole. It promises illegality, unethicalism, subjectivity, inquity, injustice, waste inefficiency and inconsistency in administrative conduct and behaviour. In addition it corrodes the faith of the common man in the legitimacy of administration and eventually undermines the idealism of those in public service and destroys the moral fabric of society. Corruption appears to be a regular universal in its pervasiveness.

India a noble country, British gave clean administration and Mahatma Gandhi gave us clean politics. This asset decepted today we are at the nadir of our fortune. The second five year plan was a major concern for public administration, it was industry oriented. The license quota system gave birth to the 'Golden Triangle' comprising politicians, bureaucrats and business men. All came closer to each other.

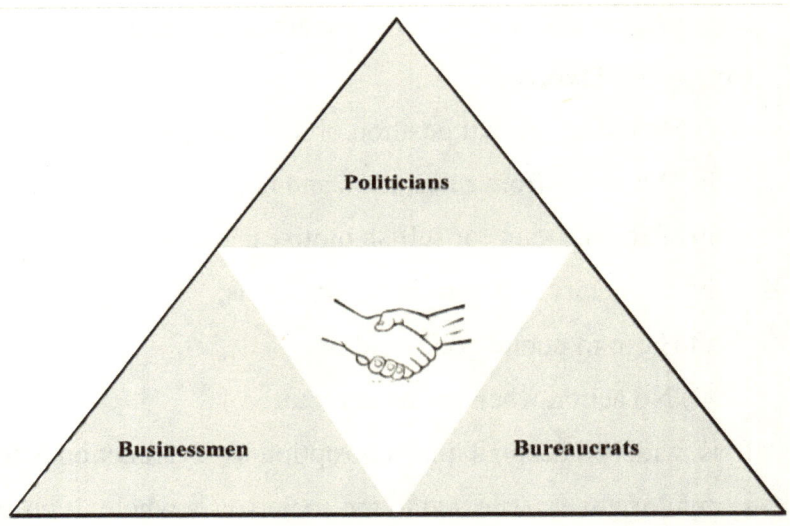

Figure 2.2
Golden Triangle of Corruption

The second five year plan proliferated government post and new posts namely 'wet post' came into play with it we lost weberian ideology. Ministers gauging the inclinations of the civil servants wanted them to bend, but they started crawling.

When we reached the end of second five year plan air was thick with corruption. This accorded primacy to lust for money and power. Small wonder, a series of scandals have besieged the Indian governmental system. The Jeep scandal, Life Insurance Corporation scandal, Bofors case, Stock scam, Sugar scandal, Telecom scandal; corruption reached all time high in 1990's with Hawala, Fodder and Cobbler scams. The Hawala was true representative of the corruption. Today with Satyam scam, Telgi scam, Commonwealth games scam, Indian coal allocation scam, 2G spectrum scam, corruption has become a multi level phenomenon from top to bottom. Centre, state and local governments seem to be involved in corrupt practices.

Central vigilance commission, in its report has identified more than thirty modes of corruption. But this list is incomplete and outmoded. The ingenuity or 'creativity' of the corrupt has multiplied the strategies of corruption in Indian public life.

The main factor responsible for this amorphous situation is the difficulty in assessing and measuring the extent of corruption in various segments and at various levels. It is equally problematic to identify the sources of corruption. The causes of corruption are as follows

- Historical causes – After World War II, scarcities led to many types of controls. It gave opportunity to resort to

35

corrupt practices and was further aggravated by the post war flush of money and consequent inflation.

- Changing values – The most important element promoting culture of corruption is the discernible erosion of ethical and moral values in public life as a result of growing materialism and consumerism in the wake of westernization, urbanization and industrialization.

- Economic causes – Remuneration of salary and scales are inadequate and the costs are rising. This is one of the reasons of corruption. It has also brought down the real income of various sections of the community. So they succumb to temptations when opportunity comes.

- Lack of strong opinion – People does not report against the corrupt officers what is more disturbing is that no stigma is attached to a person who is corrupt. This lack of sensitivity in society is more alarming.

- Nature of work – The nature of most of the departments of government is complex and complicated. It is alleged that the dilatory, cumbersome and complicate working of departments like customs and excise, imports and exports, railways, police, irrigation, state excise etc., has encouraged the practice of 'speed money' in government.

- Inadequate laws – Most of the laws of land which deals with corruption are the legacy of British and are outmoded and provide insufficient penalties.

- Undue protection to public service – The article 311 of Indian constitution, makes it difficult to deal effectively with public servants who are corrupt. There is the reluctance from higher officer for taking action against the corrupt because of their collusion with them. It has aggravated the situation.

- Elections – The two major factors which helped politician to enjoy power and clout all these years are the expansion of role of the state and the exigencies of democratic elections. The origination point of corruption in public life has been the political system. The member of political executives who comes to power enjoys substantial immunity from public accountability.

- Pressure groups – There are various professional associations, business groups, and interest groups who work like pressure groups and breeds corruption through their activities of getting favours for their community. They organise dinner, parties etc. to influence the ruling elite.

Corruption has entered every domain of India's public life and the public administration of our country is ridden with the unending series of scams and scandals which has become order of the day.

Economic Factors

According to Noble laureate economist Robbins economics is 'The science which studies human behaviour as a relationship between ends and scarce means which have alternative use.'

Population- The study of population is called demography. In terms of population, India is the second largest country next only to China. In India census takes place once in ten years.

* Growth and trends – According to the census of 1901 the population the country in that year was 23.83 crores latest census of 2011 records India's population as 121 crores.

* Causes of rapid growth of population – There are only three possible factors which results in the population increase of a country. They are high birth rate; lower death rate; and immigration

* Causes of decline in mortality rate – The causes for the lower death rate are elimination of famines, control of epidemics like cholera, small pox, decline in the incidence of malaria and tuberculosis, supplies of pure drinking water, efforts in sanitation and hygiene, spread of education, and immunization against preventable diseases.

* Causes of the high birth rate – The causes for the high birth rate are predominance of agriculture, slow

urbanisation process and predominance of rural population in India, poverty, universality of marriage, lower age of marriage, superstitions, joint family and low levels education.

Thus from foregoing analysis it should be obvious that population is impediment for development, it is not something to be eulogised and welcomed. Attempts must be made, policies should be set and bold decisions should be taken to control it, otherwise it will nullify the gains of economic growth.

Unemployment- Unemployment is a social problem which we can experience in developed economies also. It is a situation where members of the labour force wish to work but can't get job. Unemployment does not remain confined to unskilled workers only but sometimes even the skilled workers who have good training in sophisticated technologies fail to get jobs for long period. It is the manner of involuntary unemployment rather than voluntary decision on the part of an individual to choose leisure rather than work. The unemployment problem in developed and underdeveloped countries are different in nature. In developed countries, unemployment has two forms, Keynesian involuntary unemployment, and temporary frictional unemployment.

To Keynes, involuntary unemployment results from lack of effective demand. One should have to introduce effective demand and by that we can eliminate involuntary unemployment. Mostly, developed countries makes provisions for that, they provides large incentives to investors on large number on investments, resulting in the increase of effective demand. In advanced countries, technically and technologically the worker gets acquainted with the surrounding situation very fast, resulting in short frictional unemployment. The demand for labour is very less and employment opportunities are limited in underdeveloped economies where the service sector is very small with it the people who are ready to work at lower wage rates cannot get anything.

The reasons for unemployment are underdeveloped nature of economy, inadequate jobs, inadequate employment planning, rapid growth of population, increase in labour force, inappropriate technology, inappropriate educational system, etc.

Poverty- Poverty is a universal phenomenon which is found in almost all countries. It can be defined as "The members of the society who are unable to reach at the certain minimum consumption standard." It is generally agreed in this country that only they who fail to reach a certain minimum consumption standard should be regarded as poor. The concept of the poverty or the notion of the poverty is different form sector to sector and country to country. Obviously the poverty of the developed nations is different from the poverty of the underdeveloped nations because the per capita income of the developed countries is more than the underdeveloped nations. The higher class of any society possess the potential to have the luxurious life where as the subordinate class is facing the problems of basic and primary needs.

The standard of living in any society is found in two forms, absolute and relative. In the absolute standard, minimum physical quantities of cereals, pulses, milk, butter etc. are determined for a subsistence level and then the price quotations convert into monetary terms the physical quantities. Aggregating all the quantities included a figure expressing per capita consumer expenditure is determined. The population whose level of income is below the figure is considered to be below the poverty line.

In the relative standard, income distribution of the population in different fertile groups in estimated and a comparison of the levels of living of the top 5% to 10% with the bottom 5% to 10% of the population reflect the relative standards of poverty.

Causes of Poverty – The Migration of people from the rural areas in the same states is the result of the failure of development as compared to the migration. The slow growth rate in manufacturing and industrial sector results into slow rate of urbanisation in India. The socio economic structure prevailing in country side is the major cause of poverty in India. The main question before the decision makers is to remove the poverty in rural areas and major programmes are to be undertaken targeting this segment. Government introduced land reforms after the independence but it could not make effective progress in agricultural sector. The twin causes of poverty are under development of economy and inequality in the distribution of national income. Regional disparity among the various states results in uneven development and poverty. Natural calamities like flood and famines hampers monsoon based agriculture most of the people lives for sustenance on it.

Socio – Cultural Factors

Decision making takes place in context of the society. Hence just like society, decision making is concerned with values and belief systems. Science of society is concerned with the human group behaviour, the various types of groups and the ways in which they influence human instincts. The bureaucracy itself forms a distinct group while maintaining its identity it interacts with its social environment. The major components of these socio-cultural environments are as follows:

Religion- Since time immemorial religion has influenced the behaviour and way of life of individuals. It is a sum total of ideas about a particular life. Religion forms an important part of our social life. Religious ideals and values compel the members of the society to adhere to it. In religion the followers pin their faith on a super human or super natural power. Religions faith of belief controls and guides the individual behaviour. Indian society is divided along religious lines and these have varying degree of influence on the decision making. Weberianism would expect decision makers to be objective and impersonal but they are continuously exposed to forces drawing their sustenance from religion and some even succumb to it.

Caste- In every society there are certain provisions for regulation of social control and determination of individual status. In India, such provisions have been represented by the caste system. It is one of the principle sources of stratification and exercises a powerful influence upon the social structure. The caste system is not able to coordinate the vastness and complexities of modern social life. In the light of the conception of equality, liberty and fraternity, stratification and social hierarchy appears unethical. The caste system is gradually shedding its original purpose but under the impact of universal suffrage evokes new meaning and serves other purposes it has quickly emerged as a rallying point, a mobilisation device for political ends. Decision makers are increasingly getting manipulated by the caste system. Caste in Indian society refers to a social group where membership is largely decided on the basis of birth. The section comprises a local group whose members do not enter into martial relationship with outsiders. Originally this group was associated with a specific profession. The mutual relationship of one caste with the other is established on the principle of lineage and the resultant period purity of blood, making the relationship between one and other caste distant. A caste usually is fragmented into several sub-castes whose members are more unified. Each group maintains its identity and establishes relationships with similar groups spread over a large geographical area.

Caste is dominant factor in Indian public life. The general elections held in the country have been indicative of their influence. Their influence is not confined to the regions of South India which are considered to be the strongholds of caste but are equally obvious in the north. Caste through a united effort of its members to assert them, has today intruded in both politics and administration, mainly through institutions like Panchayati Raj. In every part of the country castes are trying to emerge in a big way. One should also admit that these castes also violate some of their own traditions for gaining certain common economic and political benefits. Caste as a separatist notion is a challenge to secularism but if caste creates separation, it also brings the people together as a group. Democracy increases the activities of the caste groups. Caste as the power of ruling elite gradually passes on the people in a mass society its impact. Sometimes one caste dominates over the other due to social conditions.

Caste is one such organisation with which the people are associated. The linkage between politics and caste in thus important and in the process both interact so closely that they are transformed. The caste institution is influenced in a dynamic and developing society by modernization, industrialization and urbanization.

Regionalism- India is a vast country inhabited by people of different races, speaking different languages, having many religions which are further divided into various castes, sub-castes and sects and sub-sects, geographically also it is of a continental size. Some of the ethnic religious and linguistic groups have a concentration of populations in certain areas which they regard as their own. They are primarily interested in the economic development of these and at the same time want to preserve their cultural identity, to protect their economic interest they do not want outsiders to settle there. All these factors have combined together to give birth to regionalism which takes various forms.

Linguistic regionalism is one of the most important forms of regionalism. Regionalism in its linguistic form has asserted itself in three forms. They are as follows:

- Forcing the centre to reorganise the states on linguistic basis
- Preventing the centre to make 'Hindi' the sole official language within a period of 15 years as originally provided in the constitution; and
- Committing violence against linguistic minorities within states

Though the process of linguistic reorganisation continued till 1971, even thereafter there are demands for further reorganisation of states both on linguistic and non – linguistic basis.

The existence of interstate boundary disputes and water disputes is also a manifestation of regionalism at present. This problem in the form of boundary disputes came into existence because of linguistic reorganisation of states in 1956 and thereafter. At present there are such disputes among Gujarat, Madhya Pradesh, Rajasthan and Maharashtra on Narmada waters, Karnataka and Maharashtra on Godavari waters. These territorial and water disputes have defied their solution because of sensitive feeling of regionalism.

'Sons of soil theory' is another form of regionalism unfortunately this theory has its provision in the constitution itself because it empowers parliament to make residence within the state a qualification for employment and as a result there of most of the states have enacted laws reserving jobs for the inhabitants of the state moreover special provisions for some states already accept the principle of 'sons of soil theory'. This 'son of soil' theory is spreading like wildfire because of increasing number of the educated and semi educated unemployed. Hence, the slogans, Maharashtra for Maharashtrians and so on, have become fascinating for the youth. The other factors for regionalism are demand for full statehood, demand for state autonomy, and demand for interregional autonomy within states. The economic exploitation, political domination, fear of losing cultural identity, and personal and selfish motives of politicians are some of the causes which have encouraged the spread of regionalism. Regionalism by very definition, is a trend which encourages sub nationalism when exercised without a balance, is bound to affect the unity and integrity of a nation. The regional causes are narrow based. Region directly and persistently affects the working conditions in public administration, thereby affecting morale and motivation. In India rural posting are trying ones and these creates placement problem.[4]

Language- In the case of language policy making, the official language of the Union has been laid down by the constitution of India (Article 343), which has also identified, in its eighth schedule, the various languages of the country to be used for purposes specified in Article 345 of the constitution. Further, the constitution has put an authority in the hands of the central government, both for formulation and implementing the language policy. For example, it is the responsibility of the centre to safeguard the cultural interest of the minorities and to see that they have adequate facilities for receiving at least primary education through their mother tongue (Article 350A). It is also the special responsibility of the centre to develop and spread the official language of the union (Article 351). The state governments, however, are left free to adopt either a regional language or the official language of the union for the official purpose of the state (Article 345). According to the Indian constitution education has long been (now a concurrent subject) a state subject (Article 246). From the strictly legal point of view government of India has had no authority to make any policy decision in the field of primary and secondary education. Policy statements made by the centre therefore like the national policy on education 1963 have served only as guidelines for the states with regard to the tertiary level of education. However the centre is required to coordinate and maintain standards in higher education with the adoption of the technique of five years plan and the creation of planning commission there has been a trend towards centralisation in educational policy making. The planning commission lays down broad policy with the help of various central and state authorities. Proposals regarding educational planning are submitted to it at the state level by the education departments and university at the national level by the ministry of education and the university grants commission. Responsibilities for implementation lie in the case of the state with the educational authorities of each state and in case of the centre with the ministry of education.

The chief ministers of various states are also important participants in national policy making through the conference of all the chief ministers. In the particular field of policy making concerned with the official language the role of the chief minister's conference held in 1961 accepted the government's proposal for the continuing use of English as the associate official language is endorsed and the three language formula for the adoption at the secondary stage of the education for the teaching language subjects.

There is very little scope for policy formulation at the local level in India. In the sphere of education there are some institutions mostly primary and secondary schools which are managed by district or municipal board of education. However, since most of this receives grants from the state governments, they have very little say in policy matters. Nevertheless they take into account local condition in deciding the languages to be taught and the medium of instruction. Regarding the official language in use at the local level the union government memorandum of 1956 lays down that districts having 70% or more of its population speaking a language other than the official state language should have the status of unilingual areas with that language superseding the official state language.

For decentralizing democratic form of government to be successful it is necessary that the various regional languages are developed and used in state and local administration. Responsible participation by the people in regional and local administration is possible through the regional language. A sense of alienation and at times frustration may result when the administrative machinery functions in a language alien to majority of people. The importance of indigenous language both in administration and education at the regional level was recognised early by Gandhi, who together with his support of Hindustani as the national language argued for the simultaneous use of the regional languages of India at the simultaneous use of the regional languages of India at the provisional level. The reorganisation of the states on a linguistic basis in 1956 greatly facilitated the implementation of the regional language policy at the state level. When the constitution in 1950 left the choice of the state official language to the state governments the majority of states were bilingual or multilingual and hence single language choice for official work was difficult. The 1956 redrawing of state boundaries removed this practical difficulty and the movement for adopting a dominant regional language for official purposes gather momentum. However in spite of reorganisation of states, some states like Assam remained predominantly bilingual. To protect the interest of relatively large minority groups in such state, the reorganisation commission recommended that only states in which speakers of one language formed about 70 percent or more of the total population should be considered and treated as unilingual states. Today all states in India have chosen the dominant regional language for the official purpose of the state.

India is a multilingual country and language can integrative as well as disintegrative rather than only integrative. So much so that even now there is no consensus about the national language and though the constitution has made Hindi the official language of the union it has been opposed by southern states in general and by Tamilnadu in particular. The slogan in

51

Tamilnadu is 'English ever and Hindi never.' Tamilians say that they are Indian and not Hindian. Even other states are not free from linguistic animosities. For example there is tussle between Kannada and Tamil in Karnataka, between Hindi and Urdu in U. P. and Bihar, between Hindi and Punjabi in Punjab, between Marathi and Konkani in Goa. These linguistic differences have created social tensions and hence it makes decision making difficult.

Feudal Tendencies- The Indian state is a democratic state but the society of India has feudal features. Hierarchy provides the principle for administration but the Indian society is having vertical history, which makes decision makers succumb to it. The society expects decision makers to safeguard the interest of their kith and kin. In such a Riggsian culture ascriptive value there is little scope left for weberian neutrality and impartiality. This operative societal norms and codes cast strain on the decision making.

Rural Society- Indian society is predominantly rural society. The total environment of such society is different from urban society. There is more of nearness amongst members, socio economic factor are different. Agriculture is fundamental occupation. The system of social stratification in rural community is traditional one while in urban areas new form of stratification has come into being. The rural society is less progressive as compared to urban. People here move at a slow speed and undergo social changes slowly people are more strongly attached to their social states were as in the urban they are shifted from one states to another more often and more easily. The geographical conditions and several other factors isolate village people from the outside world. Village community has the characteristic of its own. It is quite possible that these characteristics may not be found in other village societies, in spite of common geographical factors. One more reason for isolation may be that because of these villages are self dependent for a very long time and so there was no need for them to come in contact with outside world. In such societies decisions makers lack of societal understanding hampers good decision making.

Individual Factors

No other factors influence decision making as the intrinsic factors of human personality does. This may be individual abilities, experience, attitudes or personality as a whole.

Ability- Ability is an individual capacity to perform the various tasks in job. We all are not created equal. But it does not mean that some individuals are inherently inferior to others. Everyone has strength and weaknesses in terms of ability that make him or her relatively superior or inferior to others in performing certain tasks or activities.[5] Intellectual abilities are those needed to perform mental activities. The intellectual abilities play an important role in complex jobs with demanding information processing requirements. Physical abilities are required to do tasks demanding stamina, dexterity, strength and similar skills. Physical abilities are important in less skilled and more standardised work.

Experience- Experience is knowledge or practical wisdom gained from what one has observed, encountered or undergone. In decision making, which requires selection of alternative from the available alternatives, experiences of decision maker plays an important role. The successes and failures of the post which experience offers serve as guide to the future. Relying on experience in choosing alternative can be dangerous as well. As most of the decision makers fail to recognise the underlying reason for failure. Experience is a phenomenon of past and future requires new solutions. If we carefully analyse experience rather than blindly follow it and if we distil from experience the fundamental reasons for success or failure, then experience can be useful as a basis of decision making.[6]

Attitudes- Attitudes are evaluative statements or judgements concerning objects, people or events. Attitudes are not the same as values but the two are interrelated you can see this by looking at the three components of an attitude i.e. cognition, affects and behaviour. The cognitive component of an attitude

54

is the opinion or belief segment of an attitude for example 'discrimination is wrong'. The affective component of an attitude is the emotional or feeling segment of an attitude. For example "Rajesh discriminates against minorities. So I don't like him". The behavioural component of an attitude is an intention to behave in certain way toward someone or something. For example "I choose to avoid Rajesh because of my feelings about him". Attitudes, like values are acquired from parents, teachers and peer group members. We are born with certain genetic predispositions.[8] We model our attitudes after those whom we admire, fear or respect. We shape our attitudes on observation of family and friends behaviour. In decision making attitudes are important because they affect behaviour.

Needs- Individuals not only differ in their ability to do but also in their will to do. The will to do depends on strength of needs. Needs simply means something within an individual that prompts the person to act, it is some internal state that makes certain outcomes appear attractive. All individual have 'n' number of needs. All of these compete for their behaviour, but it is the highest 'strength need' at that moment leads to activity. The satisfied needs decrease in strength and freeze the will to do of individual. Needs are the reason underlying behaviour. When a need is satisfied according to Maslow, it is no longer a motivator of behaviour.[9] Needs are fountain of activity and the determinants of individual behaviour.

Values- Values are basic convictions that a specific mode of conduct or end state of existence is personally or socially preferable to an opposite or converse mode of conduct or end state of existence.[10] Values differ widely from person to person and from culture to culture. Their influence on peoples thinking, acting and behaviour is powerful. Value influences individual's perception.

i) They principally determine what he regards as right, good, worth, beautiful, ethical and so forth (Thus establishing his vocation and life goals and many of his motivations, for it may be assured that he will seek that which he deems desirable.)

ii) They also provide the standards and norms by which he guides his day to day behaviour (In this sense they constitute an integral part of his conscience)

iii) They chiefly determine his attitudes towards the causes and issues (Political, economic, social and industrial with which he comes into contact daily.)

iv) They exert a powerful influence on the kinds and types of persons with whom he can be personally compatibly and the kind of social activities in which he can engage.

v) They largely determine which ideas, Principles and concepts he can accept, assimilate remember and transmit without distortion.

vi) They provide him with an almost unlimited number and variety of moral principles which can be employed to rationalise and justify and action he has taken or is contemplating (If his stand is totally unrealistic, ludicrous or even harmful, he can still defend it on 'Principle'.) [11]

Personality- The term Personality is used in various senses but in all it means 'an integrated whole'. The term 'personality' has been derived from Latin word *'Personare'* thinkers and scholars like Dashiell Allport, Kimball Young, S. C. Warren, Drever and others have defined personality in various ways. The main theme of the definition is that personality is more or less an integrated body of habits, traits, attitudes, ideas, reactions, behavioural traits, which is manifested in social adjustments. The major characteristics of personality are:

- It is unique in each individual,
- It refers particularly to persistent qualities of an individual.
- It represents a dynamic orientation of organism to environment.
- It is greatly influenced by social interactions.
- It represents a unique organisation of persistent dynamic and social predisposition.

The structure of personality rests on following three foundations.

- Physiological structure – It includes influences of heredity, intelligence and mental traits, nervous system.
- Psychological structure – It consists of attitudes, traits, sentiments, feeling and emotions, values and ideas.
- Socio – cultural structure – It is the structure of personality which is influenced by the environment of social as well cultural factors or conditions.

In fact personality is the sum total of various factors and in decision making it leads to create a deep impact in affecting behaviour of the decision maker.

Prejudices- Prejudices determines and influence the human behaviour. They are nothing but a partisan attitude. Prejudice is an attitude which is covered by emotions and feelings and is based on stereotypes amongst legends, etc. Prejudices have the following characteristics:

- They are baseless conclusion and judgements.
- They are unfavourable feelings against other groups.
- They display the feelings and tendencies of every individual of a group against other group.
- They go on strengthening.
- In prejudices the process of rationalisation takes place
- They are generally based on past facts.

Prejudices are of the following kinds.

- Prejudices based on colour
- Prejudices based on language
- Prejudices based on odour
- Prejudices based on features of face
- Prejudices based on process and customs
- Prejudices based on culture
- Prejudices based on religion
- Prejudices based on caste
- Prejudices based on race
- Prejudices based on nationality
- Prejudices based on political and economic institutions
- Prejudices based on individual interests

Prejudices are born of general causes they are as follows.

- Psychological factors –That gave rise to prejudice are motive or self regard, self defence, maladjustment, abnormality, frustrated needs, and conditioning.
- Social factors – That govern the origin and development of prejudices are social distance, social taboos and restrictions, cultural differences, social conditions and phenomenon.

Other factors giving birth to prejudices can be historical, geographical, political and economic. Prejudices are important while considering ecology of decision making because prejudices influences individuals social behaviour.

Expectations- Expectations are the perceptions of appropriate behaviour for one's perception of the roles of others within the organisation.[12] In other words expectations define what one should do and believe other to do. For decision making to be effective expectations are to be compatible and in consonance with the organisation's goals and objectives.

Today decision making in organisation is continually influenced by the external and internal variables. Reality dictates that decision making does not take place in vacuum but is continually affected in numerous ways by changes in the society. This societal change requires greater sensitivity and flexibility in decision making than was needed ever before.

References

1) **Gaus, John M.,** *Reflections on Public Administration,* University of Alabama Press, Alabama, 1947, P. 8, 9.

2) **S. R. Maheshwari,** *Theories and Concepts in Public Administration,* Allied Publishers, NewDelhi, 1994, P. 173.

3) Government of India, Planning Commission, VIII Five year plan 1992-97 Vol. I, Delhi, 1992, P. 23.

4) **S. R. Maheshwari,** *Theories and Concepts in Public Administration; Allied Publishers,* NewDelhi, 1994, P. 12.

5) **L. E. Tyler,** *Individual differences: Abilities and Motivational Directions,* Englewood Cliffs N. J., Prentice Hall, 1974.

6) **Harold Koontz, Heinz Weihrich,** *Management,* McGraw – Hill, Singapore, 1989, P. 141.

7) **S. J. Breckler,** *Empirical Validation of Affect, Behaviour and Cognition as Distinct Components of Attitude,* Journal of Personality and Social Psychology, May 1984, P. 1191 – 1205.

8) **R. D. Arvey and T. J. Bouchard. Jr.,** *Genetics Twins and Organisational Behaviour,* in B. M. Staw and L. L. Cummings (Ed.), *Research in Organisational Behaviour,* Vol. 16, Greenwich, Ct : JAI Press, 1994. P. 66, 68

9) **Abraham Maslow,** *Motivation and Personality,* 2nd Edition, Harper and Row, New York, 1970

10) **M. Rokeach,** *The Nature of Human Values,* Free Press, New York, 1973, P. 5.

11) **Robert McMurry,** *Conflict in Human Values*, Harvard Business Review 41, July – August. 1963, P. 130-138.

12) **Paul Harvard and Kenneth H. Blanchard,** *Management of Organisational Behaviour: Utilizing Human Resources,* Prentice Hall, New Delhi, 1996, P. 162.

WHAT IS AN IMPULSE?

> *"I am convinced that an important stage of human thought will have been reached when the physiological and the psychological, the objective and the subjective, are actually united, when the tormenting conflicts or contradictions between my consciousness and my body will have been factually resolved or discarded."*
>
> Ivan Petrovich Pavlov
> Physiology of the Higher Nervous Activity (1932), 93-4

It is very much clear from our discussion that decision making is a behavioural activity as it involves a choice for best possible alternative. Individual choice making activity depends upon two vital things, facts and value. Facts though important come into play in a structured activity of organisation which is programmed because of its routine and repetitive nature. Mostly fact based decisions are taken at the lower and middle level of the organisation. Value comes into action when there is no set precedence for choice making or when a contingency arises which has not arise previously and which has not even anticipated by the planners and administrators. The value choice of the decision makers reveals his entire personality.

Now, behavioural basis of decision making is discussed in detail and how impulse comes in play and affects it.

Physiological Bases of Behaviour- In discussing behaviour we now will see the structure which enables organisms to respond (sense organs, neural mechanisms, muscles and glands), how stimuli are received, how their effects are translated into nerve impulses and stored in the brain and how reactions of these structures serve as stimuli for further events.

Individual Differences- In human beings individual differences in physical structure play an important role in many activities. Exceptionally successful sportsmen for example appear to have abnormally high lung capacity. Sir Don Bradman the legendary batsman in cricketing history is credited with unusually fine hand eye coordination and flexible wrist action. At the other end there are 'n' number of physical deficiencies some inherited and other acquired which results in behavioural differences. One example of an inherited sense organ deficiency is colour blindness. The person with these defects cannot work where fine discrimination of specific colour is required. On the contrary brain injury illustrates an acquired deficiency. Injury to certain areas of the brain may produce a condition in which a person cannot understand the meaning of words, although, able to read and hear them and was able to bring it in usage previously. Physiological differences also influence the versatility of behaviour among normal persons. It is apparent that each of us has a unique quality and that individual differences in physiological structure can extraordinarily affect behaviour.

Nervous system- It is this structure which accounts for the uniqueness of *Homo sapiens*. The nervous system is unique in the vast complexity of the control actions it can perform. It receives literally millions of bits of information from the different sensory organs and then integrates all these to determine the response to be made by the body. The supreme example of nervous, systems working is that of 'mans' which in contrast to simpler organisms, is characterised by an extensive central organisation of nerve cell along the backbone and especially in the head. This pattern and interconnected concentration of nerve cells results in wide variety of specific action which can be combined into complex behaviour pattern. Consider a person playing a 'sitar', he must respond to the technicalities of ragas which he is playing and also to the auditory impulses initiated by the accompanying 'tabla' and by his own playing and to impulses originating in the muscles of his hands and arms, all this must be fully coordinated to produce successful performance such a complex integration of sensory information and activities of muscles could not be possible without the differentiated yet integrated influence of man's complex nervous system. It is this elaborate sensory mechanism which enables a man to perform at high level of complexity which is not possible in lower animals. The human nervous system especially the highly developed brain makes people different from all other animals. The human brain functions much like a complicated computer that enables people to speak, produce creative ideas and even solve difficult problems. The nervous system provides pathway by which information travels from a person's surroundings to the brain. The brain then sends instruction to various muscles via other pathways so that the body can respond to the information. The nervous system also regulates internal functions, such as breathing, digestion and heart beat. All of a person's movement, sensations, thoughts and emotions are products of his or her nervous system. The nervous system has three main parts – The central nervous system (CNS); the peripheral nervous system; and the autonomic nervous system.

The Central Nervous System- The central nervous system functions as a main switch board that controls and coordinates the activities of the entire nervous system. The central nervous system consists of the brain and the spinal cord.

The Brain- The human brain is greyish pink, jelly like organ with many ridges and grooves on its surface. A new born baby's brain weight less than ½ kilograms. By the time a

66

person is six years old, the brain reaches its full weight of 1.4 kilograms. Most of the brain cells are present at birth and so the increase in weight comes mainly from the cells growth. A person learns and acquires new behaviour patterns at the fastest rate during this six year period in the life. Two types of cells are present in the actual substance of the brain. The basic functional unit of the nervous system is a nerve cell called neuron. The neuron is sustained and supported by the non communicating glial cell. Glial cells are known as neuroglias or glia. The vast quantity of oxygen and food required by the brain is supplied to it by a network of blood vessels. The human brain makes up only 2 percent of the total body weight, but it uses about twenty percent of the oxygen used by the entire body when at rest. The brain can function without oxygen for only three to five minutes before serious damage results.

The brain is divided into three regions, the cerebrum, the cerebellum and the brain stem.

The Cerebrum - It is the mass of nerve tissue whose broad, convex surface is closely related to the internal aspect of the calvaria, composed of the cerebral hemispheres, each made of a frontal, temporal, parietal, and occipital lobe and constituting part of the fore brain.[1] The cerebrum makes up about 85 percent of the weight of the human brain. The outermost part of the cerebrum is formed by a thin layer of nerve cell bodies called the cerebral cortex or cortex. The surface of cerebral cortex is formed by ridges and grooves. The folding growth increases the surface area of the cortex within the limited space of the skull.

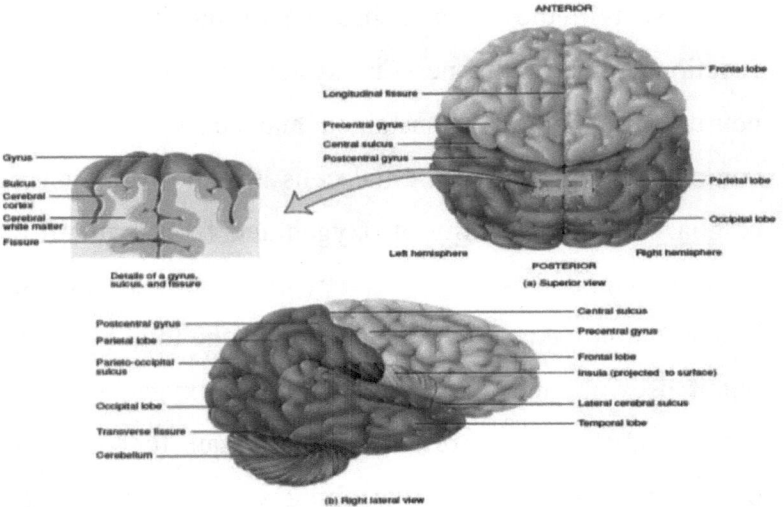

Figure 3.1
Cerebrum

The area of the cortex which receives messages from the sense organs as well as messages of touch and temperature from throughout the body is called the sensory cortex. The area which sends out nerve impulses that control the movements of all the skeletal muscles is called the motor cortex. The largest portion of the cortex is associated with analysis, processing, storing of information it is because of this higher mental activities like thinking, speaking and remembering can take place. This cortex is called as the association cortex.

The cerebrum is divided into two halves, the left cerebral hemisphere and the right cerebral hemisphere by a fissure which is a large groove, furrow or a cutting. The hemisphere are connected by bundles of nerve fibres, the largest is corpus callosum. Each hemisphere is divided into four regions called lobes. They are the Frontal lobe at the front, the temporal lobe at the lower side, the parietal lobe at the middle and the occipital lobe at the rear.

Fissures in the cerebral cortex form the boundaries between the lobes. The two major fissures are the lateral fissure and the central fissure.

The Cerebellum- The cerebellum is located below the back part of the cerebrum. The cerebellum is the part of the brain responsible for posture coordination and the balance of movement. The cerebellum is that part of the hindbrain lying dorsal to the pons and medulla oblongata, comprising a middle portion and a cerebellar hemisphere on each side.[2] The cerebellum consists of a large mass of closely packed leaf like bundles of nerve cells called folia. It has a right hemisphere and a left hemisphere which is joined by vermis which is a finger shaped structure. Pathways from the right half connect with left cerebral hemisphere and the right side of the body and pathways from the left half connect with the right cerebral hemisphere and the left side of the body.

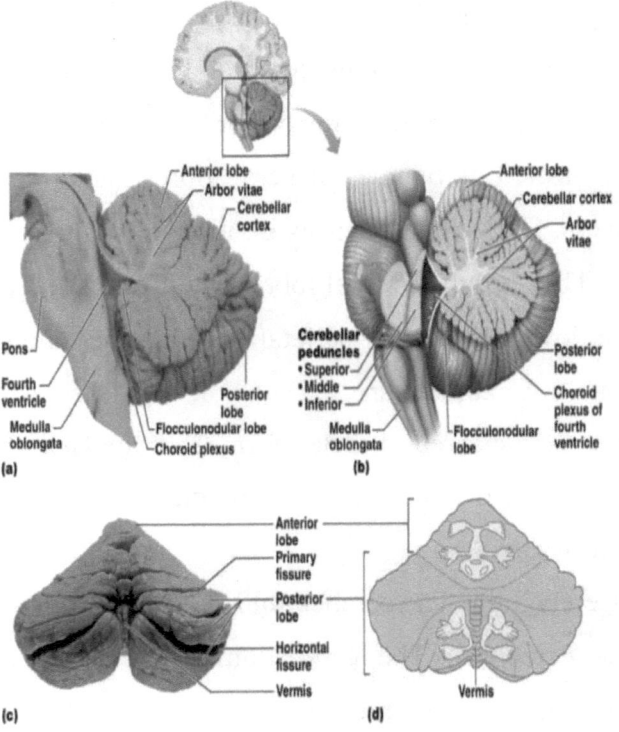

Figure 3.2
Cerebellum

The Brain Stem- It is a star like structure that connects the cerebrum with the spinal cord. The bottom part of brain stem is called medulla oblongata. The medulla has nerve centres that control breathing, heartbeat and other important body processes. The major sensory and motor pathways between the cerebrum and body cross over while passing through the

70

medulla, thus enabling the right cerebral hemisphere to control left part of the body and left cerebral hemisphere to control right part of the body. The pons which connects the hemisphere of the cerebellum is situated just above the medulla. The pons contains nerve fibers that link the cerebellum and the cerebrum. Midbrain is situated above the pons. The movements of the eye and the size of pupils are controlled by the nerve centres in the midbrain.

Thalamus and hypothalamus are at the upper end of the brain stem. Each thalamus receives nerve impulse from various parts of the body and routes them to the appropriate parts of the body and routes them to the appropriate parts of the cerebral cortex and also relays impulses from one part to the another part of the brain. The body temperature, hunger and other internal conditions are regulated by hypothalamus. The reticular formation lies deep within the brain stem it is a network of nerve fibres. Brain's level of awareness is regulated with the help of reticular formation. Sensory messages that pass through the brain stem stimulate the reticular formation which in turn stimulates activity and alertness throughout the cerebral cortex.

How Brain Works- The coordinated activities of many brain area is involved in most of the functions of the brain. The functions of many areas of the cerebral cortex have been mapped by neurologist by electrically stimulating the brain

71

during brain surgery. Brian operations do not require that the patients be unconscious because the brain feels no pain directly. Thus, the patients can tell the neurosurgeons what they experience particular area of brain are stimulated. It has been revealed in brain surgery that certain functions of the cerebrum occur chiefly in one hemisphere or the other. The operation in the cases of epilepsy produces a condition called 'split brain' in which no communication occurs between the hemispheres. The split brain studies of patients reveal that the left hemisphere largely controls our ability to use language, mathematics and logic. The right hemisphere is the main centre for visual patterns, expression of emotion, musical ability and the recognition of faces.

The chief task of cerebral cortex is to receive and interpret sensory massages. Various parts of the body send nerve impulses to the thalamus which routes them to the appropriate areas of the cerebral cortex. The somasthetic cortex which is an area of sensory cortex receives messages that it interprets as bodily sensation such as touch and temperature. It lies in the parietal lobe of each hemisphere, along the central fissure. Some reflex actions do not involve the brain, for example, if a person touches a hot stove, pain impulses flash to the spinal cord, which immediately sends back a message to withdraw the hand. However, the brain plays the important part in controlling our conscious movements as well as those we are unaware of. Deep within the cerebrum lies, basal ganglia or basal nuclei which is a collection of neurons. The unconscious movements involved in activities like eating or walking is controlled by basal ganglia, other movements of the body's involuntary muscles which line the walls of the stomach, intestines and blood vessels are controlled by the areas in the brain stem.

The cerebral cortex and cerebellum together regulate voluntary movements. The main control centres for body processes are in the brain stem. Nerve centres in medulla oblongata regulate such functions as breathing, heartbeat and blood flow. The brain stem controls swallowing and the movements of the stomach and intestines. Limbic system which is a group of brain structures plays a central role in the production of emotions. This system consists of portions of temporal lobes and parts of the hypothalamus and thalamus. Scientists have only an elementary understanding of the extraordinary complex processes of remembering and thinking. Thinking involves processing information over circuits in the association cortex and other parts of the brain. These circuits enable the brain to combine information stored in the memory with information gathered by the senses. Scientists are just beginning to understand the simplest circuits of the brain. Scientists also know very little about the physiological basis of memory. But evidence suggests that memories may be formed through the establishment of new brain circuits or by the alteration of the existing circuits. Both the process involve changes at the synapses i.e. a point where impulses pass from one neuron to another. The large molecules at the synapses, glycoproteins control these changes.

The Spinal Cord- The spinal cord is a cable of neurons that extends from the neck about two third of the way down the backbone. The spinal cord contains pathways that carry sensory information to the brain and also pathways that relay commands from the brain to the motor neurons.

The Neurons- A thin nerve membrane surrounds the entire cell. A neuron has three basic parts the cell body, the axon, and the dendrites.

The cell body- It is a ball shaped structure of neuron about 0.025 millimetres wide. Each neuron cell body receives and sends nerve impulses. The cell body also makes proteins and uses energy for the maintenance and growth of the nerve cell. The vast majority of neuron cell bodies are within the central neurons system. Those which lies outside the central nervous system are grouped into clusters called ganglia.

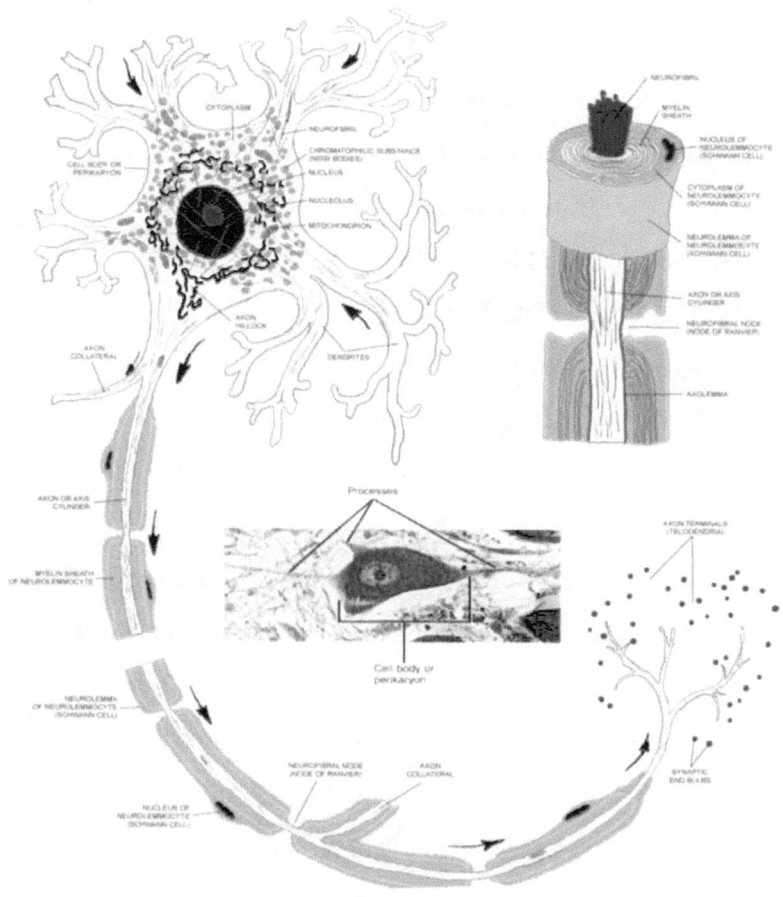

Figure 3.3
Neuron

The Axon- It is a tube like extension of a neuron cell body. It is also called as nerve fibre. The axons in all central nervous system are less than 1 mm long wide. Axons in the peripheral nervous system are longer. An axon of one neuron has enough

75

branches to make contacts with 1000 other neurons. The structure commonly called nerves, are made up of axons of motor neurons or sensory neurons or both motor and sensory neurons. Some axons are covered by myelin which is a sheath of a fatty white substance. The speed of impulses along the axons is increased by myelin.

The Dendrites- The Dendrites of a neuron are branching tube like extensions of the cell body that form a pattern resembling the limbs of a tree. Most neuron cell bodies have about six major or main dendrites. Each of which is two to three tunes thicker as the axon of the cell. The distance is about 0.5 mm between the cell body and the tips of the dendrites. Dendrites are specialized structure for receiving impulses from the axons of another neuron. Dendrites and axons do not quite touch each other. Most of the times they are separated by an extremely narrow space called the synaptic cleft, over which nerve impulses are transmitted. These places where one neuron communicates with another are called synapses.

The Peripheral Nervous System- The peripheral nervous system consists of 12 pairs of nerves that originates in the brain plus 31 pairs of nerves of the spinal cord. The peripheral nervous system carries all the messages sent between the central nervous system and the rest of the body. The nerves originating from brain and spinal cord serve as telephone wires that carry message to and from every receptor and effectors in the body.

The Autonomic Nervous System- The automatic bodily processes like breathing and digestions regulated by the autonomic nervous system without the conscious control of brain. A stable internal environment is maintained by the body due to this constant regulation. The sympathetic system and parasympathetic system are the two parts of autonomic nervous system. The actions of sympathetic nervous system includes speeding up the heart beat, sending additional blood to the muscles and enlarging the pupils of the eyes to use all available light. The parasympathetic system functions opposite of sympathetic system. It slows down the heart beat, diverts blood from the muscles to the stomach and intestine and contracting the pupils of the eyes. The balance between two is controlled by the central nervous system.

Basic Units of Behaviour

Behaviour is a gateway by which we reach out and receive inputs from environment. It is through behaviour one interacts and responds with environment. The structure i.e. receptors, effectors and neural conduction mechanism, which affects behaviour are discussed as under.

Receptors- The receptors can be stimulated by which the surrounding information is supplied to us. Receptors are microscopic structures present within the eyes, skin, ears and sensory organs. The information transmitted by the receptors is the 'first cause' of behaviour. No doubt the role of brain process is also needed for it. Some sense organs have accessory structures which helps in their smooth and effective functioning for example eye lens focuses light but it does not contain receptors. They are located in retina of eye. The receptors provide information about the outside world when external energies are acted upon them. Stimulation of receptors typically occurs at the beginning of each behaviour sequence.

Effectors- These are the organs which effects and organisms response to a stimulus. It enables and organism to do something about his environment for example to withdraw the hand from fire. In this process action is initiated by motor nerves that bring impulses and glands which results in their movements it also causes glandular secretion.

Neural Conduction Mechanisms – The activity of receptors and brain in mechanism helps man by making him aware about his surrounding environment, man than responds to his environment through his effectors. The messages than are transmitted within the body so that the individual can react. The nervous system is responsible for this transmission of message. The basic structural units for this are single living cells called neurons, which are composed of typical cell body and two types of nerve fibres axons and dendrites. Axons carry nerve impulses away from cell bodies while dendrites carry nerve impulses towards cell bodies.

Synapses- This is the region where a nerve impulse passes from one neuron to another. Synapse is a special junction where axons of nerve fibers of higher organisms end which is in very close proximity to other neurons. This region is termed as synapse. In some synapses nerve impulses are slowed up and inhibited and go no further. On the other hand an impulse entering a synaptic junction may activate many other connecting fibers, as it happens in spinal cord and brain. Sometimes, impulses which enter a particular circuit continue to travel around it. Those reverberating circuits occur at all levels of the nervous system but especially in the higher brain centres.

Reflexes- It is a response of some part of body. Reflex is simple inborn and automatic. It is an action or movement of an involuntary nature in which a stimulus is transmitted along a sensory nerve to a nerve centre and from there reflected along a motor nerve to call into play muscular to other activity.

Psychological Bases of Behaviour

After discussing the structures which enables organisms to respond which we discussed under various heads (individual differences, neural conduction mechanism). We now turn to the psychological basis of behaviour in which we are going to discuss instincts and nerve impulse.

Instincts- Instincts play an important role in animal and human behaviour. Instincts are the foundation on which human behaviour rests. When humans were not civilized they behaved according to their instincts. It is after the evolution of ages instincts got modified into a more civilized form. Basically instincts refer to pattern of behaviour which is more complex than reflexes. Instincts are present universally amongst all the species in the form of unlearned nature. It needs certain experiences or situations in which they are break out or released.

Nerve Impulse- Though it is more part of biology. Still, I have included it in psychological bases because for the activation of any impulse a 'stimuli' is necessary. It is provided for by the situation by which the impulse can be released. "A nerve fibre is supposed to be surrounded or encased in a membrane that is somewhat 'porous', or 'semi-permeable'. This means that ions (electric charges) can pass back and forth through this membrane. When the fibre is at rest, the outside is supposed to be positively charged, i.e. with a large number of positive ions on the surface of the membrane and the inside is negatively charged with a corresponding number of electrons or negative ions on the inside of the membrane. When a fibre is stimulated, it is 'disturbed' for some reason and the positive ions at the point of disturbance pass through the membrane while the negative ions come from the inside in exchange. The negative ions on the outside upset electrical balance and drive adjacent positive ions inside and more negative ions emerge into the outside systematically repeating and process, such a succession of electrical exchange is called 'depolarization'. The nervous impulse is then a series of depolarisations progressing along a nerve fibre."[3]

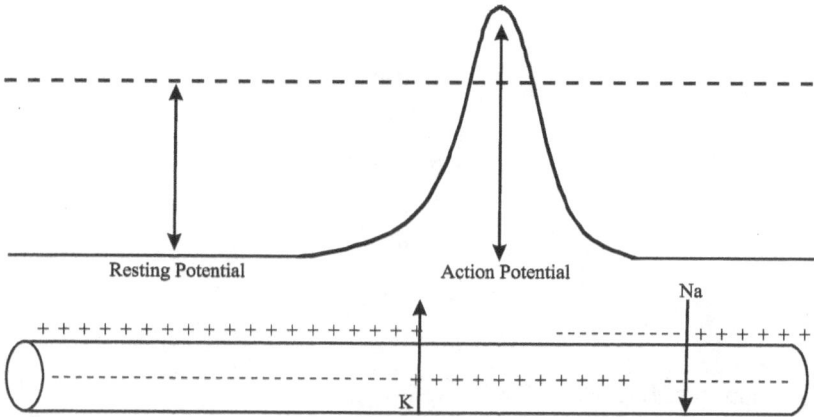

Figure 3.4
The Nerve Impulse [4]

The nerve impulse, the action potential is shown at the top (vertical dotted arrow); the nerve fibre is represented at the bottom 'during the rise of the action potential, sodium ions (Na) enter the fibre and make it positive; during the resting

81

state … the outward pressure of potassium ions (K) keeps the fibre interior negative.'

Impact of Impulse on Decision Making

Till now we discussed the complete mechanism of biological and psychological bases of behaviour including impulse.

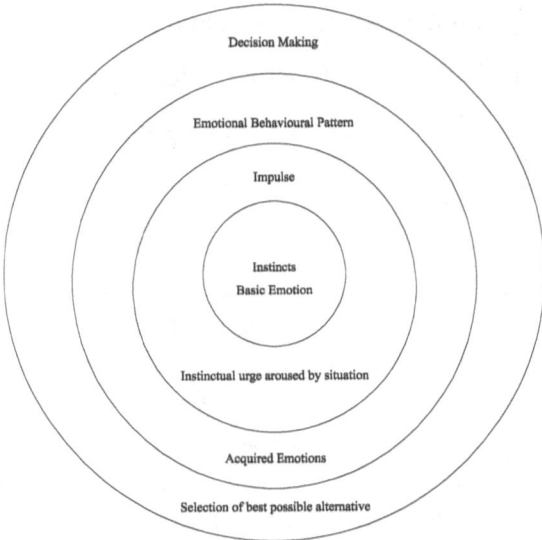

Figure 3.5
Impact of Impulse on Decision Making

Now we are going to discuss instincts, impulse, emotions, behavioural patterns which has to be dealt in comprehensive manner. The interplay amongst them will be highlighted and impact of impulse on decision making is to be seen.

Instincts- Instinct is derived from Latin word 'instincts' which means to 'instigate' or 'impel'. Instinct is an innate automatic impulse, in humans and animals which leads to a directive and

82

purposeful behaviour. Instinct is an involuntary drive or urge to act in a specific way under given condition. William MacDougull, who propounded the theory of instincts and their relating emotions that influence the human behaviour, defines instincts as "an inherited innate psycho – physical disposition which determines its possessors to perceive and to pay attention to objects of certain class. To experience an emotional excitement is particular quality upon perceiving such an object and to act in regard to it, in a particular manner, or at least, to experience and impulse to such an action."

Instincts are innate and inborn. They are found in almost all individuals in the same manner. It is possible on the basis of experience to modify and change the instincts. Although their basic characteristics remain the same, but certain changes take place in the instinctive behaviour. It is because of this that it is possible to control the instinctive behaviour. Instincts are capable of taking advantage of the past experience. It is on account of this capability that the instincts are modified and changed. All the instincts do not start functioning at the time of the birth, they grow with the development. As emotions develop so do different instincts according to biological and physical needs. Instincts are linked with emotions. Every instincts has an emotion attached to it. In fact emotion is the internal or mental aspect of an instinct. It is the instinct that basically motivates the emotions. The emotional behaviour we see is nothing but an outward possible of instinctive behaviour. Emotional experiences are in fact based on instincts. It is instincts that first arouse and then the emotions get aroused. Every instinct has some basic emotions like fear, anger, love, hunger, and shelter. It is the basic emotions possessed by instincts that generate the instinctual urge, where the arousal of instinct is situational, directly or indirectly. The instincts are prime movers of all human behaviour. Take away the instinctive dispositions with their powerful impulses, the organism would become incapable of activity of any kind, it would be inert and emotionless like a wonderful clock work, whose main spring has been removed or a steam engine with drawn out fire.

Impulse- Human impulses are not fired from the beginning by their native disposition within certain wide limits they are profoundly modified by their circumstances and their way of life. Impulse is at the basis of human activity. It is an impulse that prompts various actions. All impulse is essentially blind, in the sense that it does not spring from any prevision of consequence. In the instinctive part of our nature we are dominated by certain basis or core emotions which impulses to certain kinds of activity. Impulse is an instinctual urge.[5] Instinctive acts normally achieves some results. Impulses are sometimes defined as motives, urge, needs, wants or drives within the individual. Impulses are directed towards goals which may be conscious or subconscious. Impulses are 'whys' of behaviour. They arouse and maintain activity and determine the general direction of behaviour of an individual. In essence impulses are mainspring of action. When someone attends college, it is said that one does so because one wants to obtain education, to enjoy with friends, or to satisfy parents. When a crime has been committed, the police speculate about someone's desire for money, revenge or other personal gain. Such situation shows a common concern with impulse in human organism. Human undergo internal physiological changes related to the necessities of life such as need for nourishment and rest. The effects of these physiological changes on the nervous system prompt relevant activities. Such as eating and sleeping. These impulsive activities arise partly from the nature or internal state of the organism and they are directed towards the satisfaction of the organism in some particular way.

Impulse is a term which refers to activation from within the organism though the external stimuli may have important relationship but they do not inevitably control the organism. Impulses therefore is a general term, usually targeting to characteristics of the organism such as interests, aspirations, goals, aim, ambition and physiological states which prompt behaviour.

Emotional Behavioural Pattern- Behaviour is an externally observable activity of individual. Every action released is supposed to have an emotion attached to it, which means that all behaviour is determined by emotions which make emotions indispensable to behaviour or action. The basic emotions like hunger, feat, shelter, anger and love possessed by instincts are innate but they have been developed modified or transformed into the various subtypes or patterns of emotions with the evolution of human life, for example, the emotion of love is connected with happiness and altruism, repulsion or submission with emotion of fear. Drive for eating or diet control with emotion of hunger, emotion of shelter with ownership and acquisition, emotion of anger with rage, hatred or domination where as power, prestige, status, name, game etc. is outcome of various complex, basic and developed emotions.

In the figure 3.6 emotions which are 'basic' with their developed subtypes are depicted.

Power, Prestige, Status, Name, Fames, etc				
Love	**Fear**	**Hunger**	**Shelter**	**Anger**
Happiness	Anxiety	Eating Drive, Specific Diet, etc.	Ownership Acquisition, etc.	Revenge
Pleasure	Stress			Rage
Contentment	Depression			Aggression
Relaxation	Repulsion			Hatred
Potency	Submission, etc.			Jealousy
Self – Indulgence				Domination, etc.
Altruism				
Exhilaration, etc.				

Figure 3.6
Emotional Behavioural Pattern

The emotions which are not innate are acquired by the individual in his social structure by taking help from society. Social conditions continue to influence the individual and make them adjust accordingly. Several social conditions and institutions, for example family, education, socio economic conditions, cultural life, etc., influence the development of human emotional behaviour. Human emotions are the most complicated matter. It is directed at the achievement of certain aims and objects. Beliefs, tendencies, imitation, sympathy and all other psychological and biological emotions of individual find exhibition in the behaviour. Technically it is guided by 'biogenic and socio-genic impulses'. In other words several biological and social factors influence the human emotional behaviour.

87

Decision Making- Instincts are inborn and innate and possess basic emotions which are aroused by the situation or it is prompted by it in the form of impulse which is an instinctual urge carried for expression. It is released by the emotional behaviour of the individual. The acquired emotions are the extension of the basic emotions which are innate and lies in instinctual nature of individual guided by biogenic and socio-genic impulses. It means several biological and social factors influence the human behaviour.

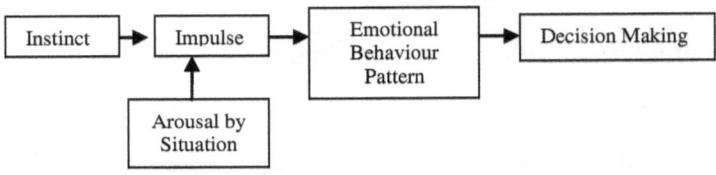

Figure 3.7
Relationship of Impulse and Decision Making

Decision making is 'reaching a conclusion' or 'making up our minds'. It is a choice making activity which selects one best possible behaviour alternative with the intention of moving towards some state of affair. It is moving towards satisfaction of impulse in decision making the totality of human behaviour is involved which creates 'impact of impulses' on decision making evident.

References

1) **Dorlands,** *Medical Dictionary,* Oxford and IBH Publishing Company, India, 1976, P. 125.

2) **Dorlands,** *Medical Dictionary,* Oxford and IBH publishing Company, India, 1976, P. 124.

3) **B. R. Bugelski,** *An Introduction to the Principle of Psychology,* Holt, Rinehart and Winston, New York, 1961, P. 143.

4) **Katz,** *The Nerve Impulse,* Scientific America, Inc, 1952.

5) **Dorlands,** *Medical Dictionary,* Oxford and IBH Publishing Company, India, 1976, P. 321.

ANALYTICS

> *"Research means going out into the unknown with the hope of finding something new to bring home. If you known what you are going to do, or even to find there, then it is not research at all, then it is only a kind of honourable occupation."*
>
> Albert Szent – Gyorgyi
>
> 'Perspectives in Biology and Medicine'

Introduction

Decision making is an act of determining over own mind upon an opinion or course of action. It is the selection based on some criteria of one behaviour alternative from two or more possible alternative. For decision making to exists, there must be two or more alternatives. If there is no choice or one choice, there is no decision to be made. The decision based on the criteria or basis believed important in particular situation and represents a choice from a group of alternatives of what one feels is the best action to be taken for particular state of affairs. It is simple to state that alternatives are evaluated in terms of their respective probable outcomes but to determine the relative merits is usually difficult. The requirement is to make comparison based on values be they economic, political, social, and religious and conflict among this values is quite likely. There are normally both desirable and undesirable aspects in every alternative but these conflicting values must be reconciled in some satisfactory manner. Many problems requiring a decision are not solved by a simple yes or no. Decision making is not a matter of 'black or white' but mostly 'grey'.

The Test

According to Morgan, the alternative to a test is natural observation of a person. The natural observation is time consuming and imprecise. It can provide enormous data after hours and hours of tedious work without telling what is important and what is trivial. As a matter of economy, people usually want to know quickly the things that are important about an individual. They need a crisp description not a book and for precision, they would like to have the description in the form of a number of numbers. But a numeral description of person's important characteristics is in itself little more than an interesting fact. To be meaningful, descriptions must be useful in making predictions about people. We go ahead and make some decisions about the people being tested. This decision making is the real purpose of testing. Decision making on the basis of test results is both necessary and legitimate if certain conditions are met:

- If the right kind of test is used to make the decision

- If the test is a 'good' test and
- If the right kind of decision is made on the basis of an available evidence not just the test alone.[1]

About the Questionnaire

The testing of the various values hidden in an individual has been explored by the questionnaire. The questionnaire is so constructed so that the scores of different values in each personality i.e. the dominant and dormant can be obtained. The questions framed in the test are divided into five broad categories of impulses i.e. political, economical, social, religious and ideal. Each value has ten questions for the purpose of reflecting above said impulses. Each question has one mark. The total questions in the questionnaire are fifty in number. There is no negative marking, higher the scores in any of the value demarcates the strong impulse of that value i.e. ten marks in social impulse indicate that individual's social impulse is stronger amongst all other impulse, provided that the score on other categories is below ten. The social impulse of the concerned individual is most likely going to affect the decision making process.

Administration of Tests

The test is administered on hundred individuals. They were asked to complete the test. The individuals were group A and B officers of Government. Some are officers of public sector enterprise while other from revenue, police, tax, education, agriculture, etc. Five sample tests are chosen from the hundred, each representing one dominant impulse from amongst the five which are included in the tests. Each one of this sample test is discussed separately and represented graphically as follows.

Individual A

The test is being administered on individual A. The scores or the result obtained are as follows:

Sr. No.	Impulse	Score
1.	Political impulse	10
2.	Economic impulse	08
3.	Social impulse	07
4.	Religious impulse	07
5.	Ideal impulse	05

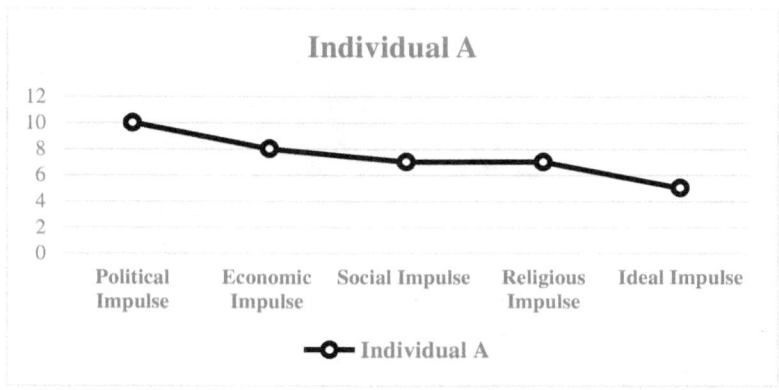

This individual's case is of a dominant political impulse as compared to the other impulse. This political impulse which is predominant in behaviour of individual 'A' may also affect his

93

decision making. The individual's routine behaviour or his choice suggests his keenness about political activities and political development taking place all around. Individual subscribes to liberty, equality, democracy, individualism, unity, diversity and have strong notions about the form, type and ideology of government.

Individual B

The test is being administered on individual 'B'. The obtained scores by the individual 'B' are as follows.

Sr. No.	Impulse	Score
1.	Economic impulse	07
2.	Political impulse	05
3.	Social impulse	03
4.	Religious impulse	04
5.	Ideal impulse	03

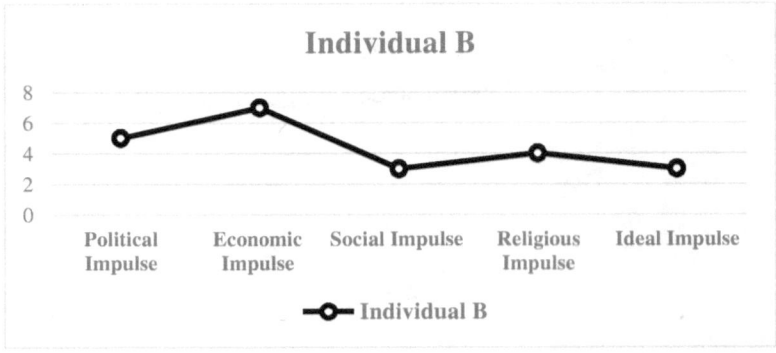

This individual 'B' is a case of dominant economic impulse as compared to other impulses. This economic impulse which is predominant may affect his decision making. The individual's

94

aptitude and routine behaviour suggest his keenness and area of choice is economic activities. Individuals have strong ideas about efficacy, speed, reliability, ease of use, flexibility, status, aesthetic appeal, emotion, cost, etc. Author Kevin Maney has also discussed this in book *'Trade-off: why some things catch on and others don't'*.

Individual C

The test is being administered on individual 'C'. The obtained scores by the individual C are as follows.

Sr. No.	Impulse	Score
1.	Social impulse	10
2.	Economic impulse	07
3.	Political impulse	06
4.	Religious impulse	07
5.	Ideal impulse	07

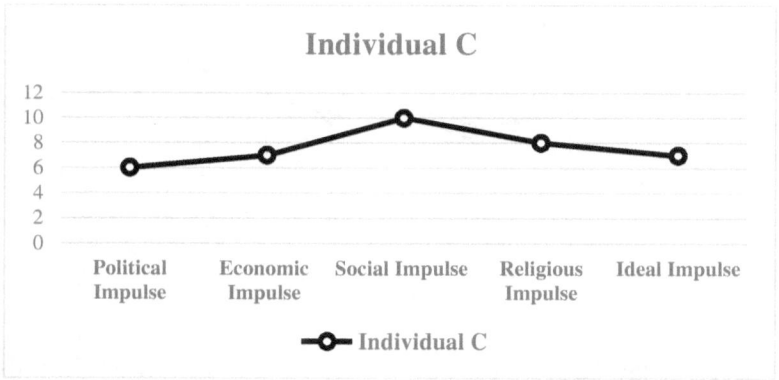

This individual 'C' is a case of dominant social impulse as compared to the other impulses. This predominant social impulse of individual 'C' may affect his decision making. The individual is a social animal taking interest in societal issues and social activities. Individuals feel strong on issues of family, community, responsibility, social commitment, social evils, customs, traditions, etc.

Individual D

The test is being administered on individual 'D'. The obtained scores by the individual 'D' are as follows.

Sr. No.	Impulse	Score
1.	Religious impulse	10
2.	Social impulse	06
3.	Economic impulse	05
4.	Political impulse	07
5.	Ideal impulse	06

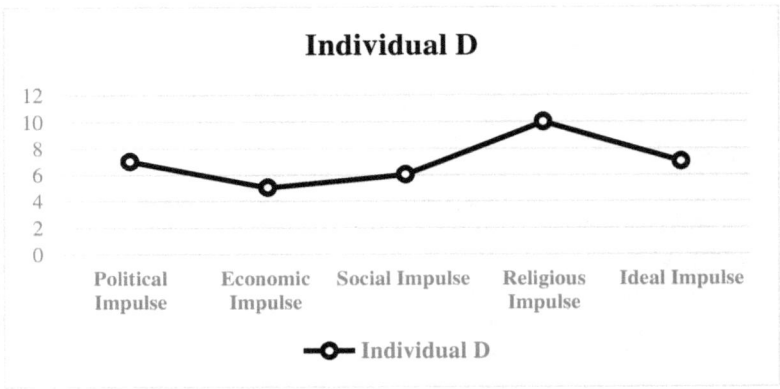

Individual 'D' is a case of dominant religious impulse as compared to other impulses. Individual 'D' shows high score on the religious impulse. This predominant religious impulse of individual 'D' may affect his decision making. These individuals are deeply religious personality with indomitable faith in precepts of religion it is evident from regular behaviour and preferences in the test.

Individual E

The test is being administered on individual 'E'. The results of the test showed the following picture. This individual has scored very high on the ideal impulses as compared to the other impulses. Individuals believes in efficiency, effectiveness, economy, responsibility, responsiveness, goal orientation, peoples participation, transparency, morals, etc

Sr. No.	Impulse	Score
1.	Ideal impulse	09
2.	Religious impulse	05
3.	Social impulse	05
4.	Economic impulse	04
5.	Political impulse	06

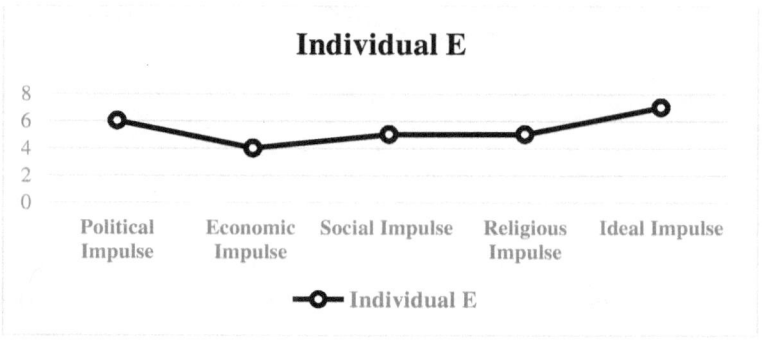

This predominantly high ideal impulse personality may even come in his decision making process and affects it. The individual's preferences on ideal and perfectionist, rational attitude is evident from his selection of answers in the test administered on him.

Overall Analysis

The test is being administered on hundred individuals all professional administrators. The inference from the tests shows the following scenario.

Sr. No.	Impulse	Score
1.	Political impulse	90
2.	Economic impulse	60
3.	Social impulse	80
4.	Religious impulse	75
5.	Ideal impulse	80

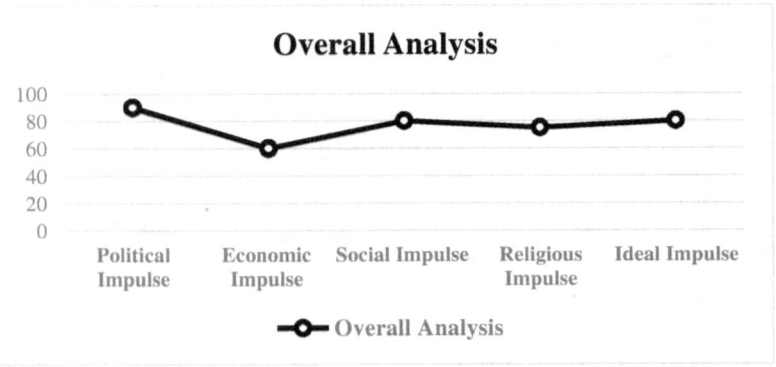

The political impulse tops the list with ninety people showing high score on political impulse. This does not mean that the rest are distributed amongst other ten. But is a fact that there are individuals who have more than one dominant impulse. The overall analysis of the scores of test administered on hundred individuals is represented graphically.

The Perspectives

Political- At the time of independence we were fortunate because Mahatma Gandhi gave clean polity whereas British gave us an efficient bureaucracy. But in subsequent years in a drive for power all virtues disappeared in thin air in the oblivion. Politics though mostly abused became the easiest way for interest aggrandisement. People aligned with politician who protected their interest by giving the administrator plump wet posts, who in turn is supposed to do favour for the political party and their men. Such administrators have dominant political impulses, they join hands with men in power and by it both gets benefitted. Due to these politicised administrators transfers in services has become order of the day when government changes, the administrators are also replaced by the incumbent politician's men. In all these officials political impulse is dominant is also evident from the results of the tests administered on some such officials.

Vanity manifest in many forms one is humanity said Plato. It is true for politicians who come to power by promising populist measures like Rs. 2 per kg rice, prohibition, etc. without taking into account the status of state's coffers. They by their speeches mesmerises the people who are unaware of the practical concern faced by the government due to paucity of funds. It is because of the strong political impulse of the politicians who forms the government and overrides all other economic, social, practical concerns and inaugurates the populist policies with lot of publicity only to abandon it in half a way.

One more case which is common in Indian context where political impulse is dominant is of the role played by officers in elections weather it may be for lok sabha, state legislatures or for local bodies. At the time of elections the officers are supposed to conduct themselves in non partisan manner. But this always is not the case. Many cases and observation can be cited in these regards where the officers acted in partisan manner.

Public policy is a concept now much in vogue. It is frequently used term in our daily life and in our academic literature where we often make references to the health policy, education policy, wage policy, agricultural policy and so on. While public policy initially emanates from the state institution both local and central governments.[2] The public servants or the senior bureaucrats are involved intimately in formation of policies. Policies are chosen under the influence of values. Decision makers often act on the basis of their belief or perceptions of the public interest concerning what is proper or morally correct public policy. Studies of the supreme courts shows that the judges are influenced by policy values in deciding cases.[3] In theory, civil servants are expected to implement the policies or decisions of the political executive. But in formulation of policy as well, it is widely established that due to the practical concern it is very difficult to maintain politics – administration dichotomy. It is widely accepted that old politics – administration dichotomy was an artificial one and that the higher civil servants exercise a great deal of influence on policy because of their administrative knowledge, permanence and closeness to political power.[4] Because of these senior bureaucrats exerts influence in formulation of policies through selective interpretation of data through their own programmers designs and strategies and through active campaigning. By doing this, the senior civil servants are able to modify, rearrange and can even change the intent of legislative enactments. Thus senior administrators extensively involved in policy making process also show a high rating on political impulse.

Economic- The principle of economy is fundamental to economics. In words of Wickstead, a famous economist, "Economy is administration with a minimum of waste," to Lord Robbins, "The criterion of economy is the securing of given ends with the least means." The criterion of efficiency as applied to administrative decisions is strictly analogues to the concept of maximisation of utility in economic theory. It is not asserted that the criterion of efficiency does dominate administration in their decisions, but rather that, if they were rational it would. The problem of administrative decisions can be translated into a problem in the theory of production and concepts and theorems developed in economic theory have wide applicability in administrative decisions. The problem of efficiency is to find the maximum of a production function with the constraint that some expenditure is fixed …that portion of the decision making process which is factual resolves itself into the determination of production functions of administrative activities …the concept of efficiency involves an analysis of the administrative situation into a positive value element (the results to be attained) and negative value element (the cost). For the practical execution of this analysis a technique is needed that will enable the administrators to compare various expenditure alternatives in terms of results and costs.[5] The administrators cost benefit analysis has necessarily to be broader, taking particular care to take into account the social cost and benefit. The application of cost benefit analysis is always not without difficulties in public administration. As Willoughby says, "The impression is widespread that it is inherently impossible to secure a same efficiency and economy in administration of public affairs that can be secured in the conduct of private undertaking."[6] It is argued that as compared to private enterprises public administration lacks incentive to efficiency and economy due to element of 'profit'. But Willoughby himself points, "Even granting that the element of incentive is absent in government enterprise, it is an open question whether it is not more than counter balance by the sentiment of public service ..... The fact that they were engaged in public service has given the personnel an *esprit de corps* and desire to excel often lacking in private enterprises and is mostly if not quite, as strong an incentive to efficiency as the production of profit." It should be noted that profit motive is not entirely absent in public administration, but is respectably accepted from the advent of government in business. The purely efficiency approach should not degenerate into mechanical efficiency. The administrators who compare various expenditure alternatives in terms of results and costs rated high on economic impulse. In a country like ours and many other developing countries the biggest challenge is to take task of rapid economic development so as to lift the country from unemployment, poverty and illiteracy. The development administrators are familiar with economic development strategy. An academic training is not indispensable to the senior civil servant. Prof. Cairncross feels that, 'it is important to find a man with the right gifts and trust him to work out the theory for himself. To a mature and experienced man with an eye for the ways of the world, there is nothing very abstruse about economic theory: certainly not about those parts of the economic theory that are truly operational and bear upon the real dilemmas of policy'.[17] According to Prof. Cairncross what is more important is the capacity to understand what figures mean and how to use them. The civil servant having this capacity had rated high on economic impulse. 'There is hardly anyone from a petty clerk to a minister who is not manageable with a proportionate amount of gratification.'[8]This holds good in all domain of public life in today's India. Corruption may be defined as the deliberate and international exploitation of one's position, status, or resources, directly or indirectly for personal aggrandisement, whether it be in terms of material gain or enhancement of power, prestige or influence beyond what is legitimate or sanctioned by commonly accepted norms to the detriment of the interests of other persons or the community as a whole.'[9] Once occupation comes to be practised on a large scale, it soon becomes the order of the day. Today, corruption is so rampant that is dominates direct dealings with the public departments such as the police, income tax, sales tax railways, imports and exports, public works, food and civil supplies are plagued by this disease. Civil servants actually rely on bribes and illegal payments. The person suffers in such case is a common man. The civil servants with tainted record, on whom the stigma of corruption is attached, who have used their office for the personal aggrandisement also rated high on economic impulse.

Social- Society is a human institution and for orienting it either for political setup or for any great change it is necessary to find solutions to the problems befitting the nation. In India, unfortunately, the colonial powers did not pay much attention to the social problems of the country. Their attitude towards the problem of India had been that of a spectator who would look at them, sometimes with indulgence and sometimes with indifference. The virtue of helping others is greatly valued in Indian culture. Kautilya's Arthashastra refers to the constructive works for the public good by the joint efforts of the villagers. It also refers to the social work like care and provision for orphans, the old or the diseased, in case they have no sympathetic guardian or protectors. In today's context problem concerning village community should be taken up. Among the villages old conservatism persists and religion is still one of the most important factors which influence their outlook and thinking. They are illiterate they do not know anything about child care way back because of the recommendation made by the child programme committee, government started providing midday meals during school hours and also started educating the parents with regard to nutrition of the children. The second most important problem of village community is education, schools have been set up in the villages but proper type of attention and encouragement is not provided to the children. The recreational facilities are not available in the villages. The only recreation in villages is consumption of wine and celebrating festivals. The woman is the cradle of civilization and also the motivation behind progress because the children get their first lesson in education from the mothers. In villages particularly their education, their health and their economic emancipation has been completely neglected. Parents do not consider daughters equal to their sons and the husbands take them to be slaves. Till she is given an equal status, she cannot serve the nation properly. The progress for welfare of weaker sections includes various measures such as provision of education, employment opportunities and the distribution of surplus land. The schemes for housing include housing for industrial workers, housing for the low income groups, housing for private enterprises and slum clearance schemes. The aim of these schemes is to make them to work is in the service of the humanity and the nation and also to develop their own personality for their personal and social benefits.

Administration in India has to pay special attention to antipoverty programmes and the problems of reaching out to the poor in both urban and rural areas. The administration is currently shifting focus on grass roots by utilizing common resources, enhancing people's access to vital developmental inputs, mobilising people's power, organizing the target groups and innovating new forms of social organizations more conducive to people centric development. This marks a radical shift from people as beneficiary, to people as an actor kind of administrative situation. In such a scenario civil servants functions, rather their came a major shift in their functions after independence from revenue collection, to developmental administration. In these changed roles they are supposed to be the social engineers who have to take along various voluntary groups and people with them for the development of the country. This may be the reason why most of the bureaucrats rated high on the social impulse. They have to be social and matured enough to take into account the social dynamics while working in administration. Noorjahan Bawa points out, "Peoples participation in the development process means active cooperation and involvement of the general masses and the targeted public in the various interfaces of the decision making

107

process in development administration. This calls for their active interest, enthusiasm and cooperation in planning, implementation and evaluation of development programmes at different levels, particularly at the grass root level."[10] It is evident from the test administered on a senior officer who had good reputation of working on developmental programmes like provision of drinking water, education rated high on social impulse.

Religious- There are two types of values, categorical or absolute values and instrumental values. The first refers to beliefs and practices in the supernatural powers. The other refers to norms and practices related to work efficiency, productivity, etc. Religion falls in the first category of the value system. Religion may be defined as 'beliefs and practices related to supernatural entities, spirits and powers, which are considered ultimate in shaping human relations.' Religion has played an important part in Indian society from the earliest times. India has been a poly-religious society, some of them are indigenous, and other has come from outside and drawn followers.

The direct impact of all religions remains healthy, elevating and socializing. Its indirect effects have been dysfunctional. An officer who is rated high on religious impulse is known for his uprightness when a questionnaire is administered on him. It may be because religion disciplines human behaviour in terms of sacred and profane. It gives a sense of collectivism and provides the model for living. Religion specifies the acts to be done or not to be done. Then is a possibility that law of karma, the fear of retribution and such other prescriptions have always an impact on human action.

Ideal- 'The work of the government would never be done if there were only the secretaries of state and other heads of departments, the presidents of boards, parliamentary under secretaries, junior lords and civil lords in other words the ministers to do it. These people cannot be expected to collect taxes, audit accounts, delivering mail, and carrying massages. Such manifold tasks fall rather to the body of officials and employees known as the permanent civil servants ….. It is this great body of men and women that translates law into action from one end of the country to the other and brings the national government into its daily contacts with the rank and file in country less in the public eye than the ministry: this army of functionaries is not a whit less necessary to the realisation of the purpose for which the government exists.'[11] Such is the significance of bureaucracy in modern government. A rapid transformation has taken place in the approach to the bureaucracy. The old 19th century negative approach has been replaced by a more positive one which creates a positive motivation that enables the civil servants to give their best to the public service. 'The new administrator has to be action minded to the point of even becoming aggressive to push the schemes through, human relations oriented, i.e., caring more for the people than for the regulations and procedures; dynamic, i.e., not content with merely pushing the files; public spirited, i.e., yearning always for the public interest; and persuasive, i.e., able to win public approval, consent and cooperation.'[12] Now the traditional concept of neutrality has been challenged with the state engaged in planned development for the welfare society the needs is to have special type of official. 'The successful carrying out of task of both types development and democratization, requires on the parts of the administrators not only the qualities of initiative, leadership and taking of responsibility, but also an emotional and intellectual integration into what may be called democratic social values.'[13] For the effective and efficient implementation of programmes what is needed is a sense of emotional integration with the programme and identification with the interest of the common man, which is not possible for a indifferent or neutral civil servant. 'How on earth can a senior government official avoid emotional attachment to policies of any administration? For grown up men working on matters like these, the avoidance of emotional attachment is nonsense ...a senior civil service that took literally what Hoover commission has said about political neutrality would be a pool of eunuchs, a special breed of Americans who stay out of trouble by staying out of sight. No political executive in his right mind would want one of them assigned to his office. A government stuffed with people who avoided emotional attachment would be like hospital full of doctors and nurses who did not care whether their patients lived or died, just so that proper professional procedures were followed …too much emphasis would shift the whole government into neutral.' Striking a right balance is necessary in the aspect of Ideal impulse. In respect of political activities, in a democratic society it is desirable for all citizens to have voice in the affairs of the state and for as many as possible to play an active part in public life and the public interest demands the maintenance of political impartiality in the civil service and of confidence in that impartiality as an essential part of the structure of government.'[14] The officers who are rated high on ideal impulse are held as best professional administrators amongst their peers and critics alike. This is because they have clarity of vision, far sightedness, unerring judgement and good conscious.

References

1) **Morgan and King,** *Introduction to Psychology*, TMH Edition, New Delhi, P.433.

2) **R.K. Sapru,** *Public Policy: Formulation, Implementation and Evaluation, Sterling* Publishers, New Delhi, 1998, P. 1.

3) **Glendon Schubert,** *Judicial Policy Making,* Foresman, Chicago, 1965.

4) **B. Heady,** *British Cabinet Ministers,* Allen and Unwin, London, 1972, P. 158, 159.

5) **Herbert Simon,** *Administrative Behaviour,* Chapter IX Criterion of Efficiency, Third Edition, the Free Press New York, 1978.

6) **Willoughby. W. P.,** *Principles of Public Administration*, Washington D.C. Brooking Institute, 1927.

7) **A. N. Cairncross,** *Factors in Economic Development,* George Allen and Unwin, London, 1962.

8) **Chaudhari Nirad C.,** *Corruption in Indian Politics*, in Public Administration, (Kanpur), Vol. 6, No. 8, August 1968, P. 20.

9) **Avasthi and Maheshwari,** *Public Administration,* Laxmi Narain Agarwal, Agra, 1997, P. 407.

10) **Noorjahan Bava,** *Peoples Participation in Development Administration in India,* Uppal Publishing House, New Delhi, 1984.

11) **Frederic Austin Ogg,** *English Government and Politics,* New York, The MacMillan Company, 1947, P. 202.

12) **Avasthi and Maheshwari,** *Public Administration,* Laxmi Narain Agarwal, Agra, 1997, P. 283-284.

13) **Lall. S.,** *Civil Service Neutrality,* I.J.P.A., Vol. IX, No.1, Jan – Mar, 1958, P. 4, 5.

14) Report of the committee on the political activities of civil servants (chaired by Mr. J.C. Masterman), London, H.M.S.O. (C.M.D. 7,718), June, 1949, P. 12.

CONCLUSION

> *"I am slowly coming to the conclusion that it's more important to learn to work with what you've got, under the circumstances you've been given, than wishing for different ones."*
>
> -Charlotte Eriksson

Conclusion

The development implies the competence of a social system to define or redefine its environment. "Environmental factors in general and cultural factors in particular, are important to those who attempt to bring about major change in a society. Such factors condition the outcome of any governmental program or other innovation. Therefore changes in man's culture and environment are among the goals of highest priority in the country's most committed to change."[1] The administrative system in the society interact with polity, economy, society, culture and all these systems 'enter into transactions with their environments, influencing and being influenced by them.'[2] Any administrative system is affected by needs and demands from the environment, which in turn are defined and redefined by the results of the working of the administrative system. Public bureaucracies are basic institutions in any society. It is

114

important because of this reason to view or deal bureaucracy in the context of it's inter- relationship with other societal institution. In systemic terms, the bureaucratic system is continually interacting with – i.e., affected by and feeding back upon – the political economic and socio-cultural subsystems in a society.[3] This interaction has a modifying impact and affects the bureaucracy. The importance attached to ecology was emphasised by scholars like John M. Gaus'.[4] Robert A. Dahl,[5] Rosce Martin,[6] and Fred W. Riggs.[7] From these perspective, administrative process may be viewed as a system having an environment with which it interacts and in which it operates.[8] This proposition is a corollary of the view that the 'larger society' is a 'system containing administrative institutions as a subsysttem'.[9]

"The function of the civil service in the modern state is not merely the improvement of government; without it, indeed, government itself would be impossible …its numbers are a measure of the activities of the state and an indication of its measure".[10] "The civil service of India, which in origin was little more than revenue collecting agency, gradually took upon itself a very wide range of duties as the work became specified, new services had to be created … India looks to government to do many things which in the west are done by private enterprise."[11] With the adoption of the concepts of welfare state and socialistic pattern of society, the sphere of government has expanded enormously resulting in an immense increase in the magnitude of administrative services.[12] It is of multipurpose character. It is composed of 'generalist administrators' who are expected from time to time to hold posts involving a wide variety of duties and functions: for example, maintenance of law and order, collection of revenue, regulation of trade commerce and industry, welfare activities, development and extension work, etc.[13]

Public administration is the machinery used by the service state to place in a position to make plans and programmes that can be carried out and to carry out the plans and programmes it has made.[14] In changing world context public administration's "purposes have been completely reoriented, its functions have enormously increased in number, variety and complexity and its methodology has grown from the trial and error stage into an orderly discipline with an organised, ever-increasing body of knowledge and experience."[15] Public administration is "organisation and direction of human and material resources to achieve desired ends."[16] Public administration "is determined action taken in pursuit of conscious purpose. It is the systematic ordering of affairs and the calculated use of resources, aimed at making those things happen which we want to happen and simultaneously preventing development that fail to square with our intentions. It is the marshalling of available labour and materials in order to gain that which is desired at the lowest cost in energy, time and money."[17] Public administration is 'the direction, coordination and control of many persons to achieve some purpose of objective.'[18] According to Herbert Simon, 'In its broadest sense, administration can be defined as the activities of groups cooperating to accomplish common goals'[19]

Decision making is at the centre of any human action. Decision making is at the core of administration. Decision is fundamental to organism and organisational behaviour. Decision making involves 'what, who, when, where, and how'. Decision making is a choice activity. Decision making involves selection of best possible alternative from the available alternatives. Decision making cannot take place when there is only one alternative option available for selection. The choice activity in decision making in turn depend upon two important factors, fact and value. The selection of best possible alternative is determined by the fact or the value. The fact value dichotomy is very abundantly available in the literature of decision making and dealt extensively by the scholars on the subject is redundant now. With the advent of the adherents of the phenomenological approach much stress is laid on the 'value' factor of choice making. The phenomenalists believe that it is the 'values' that determine the selection of facts. If viewed in these perspectives the ills of public administration like circumlocution can be attributed to it. The 'babus' are the sad despair of the Indian administration. They get sadistic pleasure in harassing the public. The 'babus' though from the part of lower and middle level public administration and engaged in the work of routine and repetitive nature takes considerable time in taking decision even when the facts are available. Values are the basic convictions. Values have judgemental content. Values carries individual's notion about what is right or what is preferable. This value judgement plays significant role in decision making. The substantial number of values is innate and the rest are acquired. Impulse which is the instinctual urge determines the value system of individual substantially. Instinct is a psycho-physical disposition innate in individual which impels to act in a specific way. Instincts are linked with emotions. Emotions in fact are mental or internal aspect of an instinct. Instincts motivate the emotions resulting into the emotional behavioural pattern. The impulses are the carriers of instinctual urge, which give rise to emotional behavioural pattern. The selection of the possible behavioural pattern is decision making. These are the behavioural impact which impulse creates on the decision making in administration.

There will be an agreement amongst the administrators that the most effective decision takes the form of comparison with the other correct decision. The question arises when administrators don't agree on the values and objectives. Then what is the test of good decision. It should be remembered that the achievement of the objectives cannot be the only yardstick for judging the decisions goodness because the ultimate validity of objectives rest on its degree of agreement amongst all players. Hence agreement only is the practicable test of decisions correctness. The decision makers have to seek to win over others to agreement on ends. It is irrational on our part to say that decision with dominant 'so and so' impulse is good or bad unless we in reality able to particularize what it is good or bad for.

Administration is now so vast an area that a philosophy of administration comes close to being a philosophy of life.[20] The situation in the arena of decision making is more complex as it involves the decision maker and the situation, which is very difficult to predict. The manifold activities of public administration and increased demands of the people expect from the decision maker to put in the words of Auguste Volmer, "The wisdom of Solomon, the courage of David, the strength of Samson, Passions of Job, the leadership of Mosses, the kindness of good Samaritan, the strategical training of

Alexander, the faith of Daniel, the diplomacy of Lincoln, the tolerance of Carpenter of Nazareth and an intimate knowledge of every branch of natural, biological and social sciences!"

All actions are impulsive action and all decisions are impulsive decisions. They are patterned or released to fulfil the instinctual urge, be it political, social, economical, or so on, what is needed from a decision maker is a positive approach from a sound and healthy mind, a diagnostic vision for perceiving things as it is and as it should be. A good developed personality is required for taking decision by considering all the ramifications holistically in the decision making ecology.

References

1) **Weidner,** *The Elements of Development Administration,* Durham, N.C. Duke university press, 1970, P. 8.

2) **Riggs,** *Idea of Development Administration,* P. 34.

3) **Ramesh K. Arora,** *Comparative Public Administration,* Associated Publishing House, New Delhi, 1990, P. 105.

4) *The Ecology of Government,* in Reflection in public administration, University of Alabama Press, 1947, P. 1-19.

5) *The Science of Public Administration,* Public Administration Review, VII, 1947, P. 1-11.

6) *Technical Assistance: The Problem of Implementation,* Public Administration Review, XII, 1952, P. 266.

7) **Riggs,** *Administration and the Ecology of Public Administration,* Asia Publishing House, Bombay, 1961.

8) **Riggs,** *Administration and the Ecology of Public Administration,* Asia Publishing House, Bombay, 1961.

9) **Riggs,** *Administration and the Ecology of Public Administration,* Bombay, Asia Publishing House, 1961.

10) **Finer H.,** *Theory and Practice of Modern Government,* P. 791.

11) Report of the Indian Statutory Commission; 1930, Vol. I, P. 263.

12) **Avasthi and Maheshwari,** *Public Administration,* Laxmi Narain Agarwal, Agra, 1997, P. 427.

13) **Avasthi and Maheshwari,** *Public Administration,* Laxmi Narain Agarwal, Agra, 1997, P. 435, 436.

14) *A Handbook of Public Administration,* United Nations, New York, 1961, P. 5.

15) *A Handbook of Public Administration,* United Nations, New York, 1961, P. 4.

16) **Pfiffner, John M., and Presthus, R. Vonce,** *Public Administration,* Ronald Press, New York, P. 3.

17) **Marx, Fritz Morstein, (Ed.),** *Elements of Public Administration,* Prentice Hall of India, New Delhi, 1964, P. 4.

18) **L. D. White,** *Introduction to the Study of Public Administration,* MacMillan Company, New York, 1958, P. 2.

19) **Simon, Smithburg and Thompson,** *Public Administration,* Alfred A. Knopf, New York, 1950, P. 3.

20) **Dimock, Marshal E.,** *A Philosophy of Administration,* Harper and Brothers, 1958.

www.ingramcontent.com/pod-product-compliance
Lightning Source LLC
Chambersburg PA
CBHW021409170526
45164CB00002B/565